AF479999

Dynamics of Retail: A Multidimensional Examination of Mechanisms, Challenges, and Opportunities in Modern Retail

In-depth Analysis of Innovations, Emerging Trends, Competitive Strategies, and Case Studies of Successes and Failures in the Retail Sector

GDO Modern

1. **History of Retail**

2. **Types of Structures** (Hypermarkets, Supermarkets, Discount Stores, etc.)

3. **Retail Geography** (Location, Concentration, etc.)

4. **Technological Evolution** (E-commerce, Apps, Self-Checkout, etc.)

5. **Logistics and Supply Chain**

6. **Stock and Warehouse Management**

7. **Merchandising and Store Layout**

8. **Private Label vs. Name Brands**

9. **Pricing Strategies**

10. **Marketing and Advertising**

11. **Customer Loyalty** (Loyalty Programs, Reward Cards, etc.)

12. **Consumer Behavior Analysis**

13. **Corporate Social Responsibility** (Sustainability, Ethics, etc.)

14. **Human Resource Management**

15. **Supplier Relationships**

16. **Regulations and Compliance**

17. **Internationalization and Globalization**

18.   **Crises and Opportunities** (COVID-19, Other crises, etc.)

19. **Product Innovations**

20.   **Packaging and Labeling**

21. **Waste Management and Recycling**

22.   **Future Trends and Perspectives**

23.   **Competition and Differentiation**

24.   **SWOT Analysis of Retail**

25.   **Case Studies and Success Stories**

26.   **Failures and Lessons Learned**

27.   **Role of Emerging Technologies** (Blockchain, AI, etc.)

28.   **Impact on the Local Community**

29.   **Business Models and Competitive Strategies**

30.   **Customer Service and Complaints Management**

1. The History of Retail

The history of retail is vast and diverse, intertwining with the socio-economic evolution of the world over time. Here's a basic overview:

History of Retail 1. Origins:

- Late 19th Century: The origins of modern retail can be traced back to the late 19th century with the opening of the first department stores in the United States and Europe.
- Early Department Stores: Le Bon Marché in Paris, Harrods in London, and Macy's in New York are examples of pioneering retailers in this sector.

2. Expansion and Diversification:

- 1920s and 1930s: The first supermarkets and discount stores emerged.
- Post-World War II: Retail experienced significant expansion, especially in the United States, with the rise of shopping malls and supermarket chains like Walmart.

3. Globalization:

- 1980s and 1990s: Retail chains began expanding globally. Walmart, Carrefour, and Tesco became global brands.

- Entry into Emerging Markets: Retail giants began entering Asian, South American, and African markets, adapting their business models to local cultures.

4. Technological Evolution and the Internet:

- Late 1990s and early 2000s: The advent of the internet gave rise to e-commerce. Amazon became a major player in online retail.
- Evolution of Online Platforms: Various forms of e-commerce developed, including online-to-offline (O2O) and mobile commerce (m-commerce).

5. Sustainability and Social Responsibility:

- 2010s: Increased focus on sustainable and responsible practices. Initiatives to reduce environmental impact and promote social responsibility gained traction.
- Certifications and Standards: Certifications and standards became widespread to ensure product quality and ethical production.

6. COVID-19 Pandemic and New Trends:

- 2020-2021: The COVID-19 pandemic accelerated the digitization of retail and altered shopping habits, emphasizing the importance of e-commerce and home delivery services.

- Innovations and Changes: New technological solutions, such as augmented reality for online shopping and supply chain tracking applications, emerged.

7. Future Perspectives:

- Emerging Technologies: Blockchain, Artificial Intelligence, and the Internet of Things (IoT) are among the technologies expected to shape the future of retail.
- New Business Models: Explorations into new business models, such as the circular economy and personalized offerings, are ongoing.

The history of retail is undoubtedly a complex and fascinating mosaic of progress, innovations, and adaptations. From the humble beginnings of the first department stores, it has evolved into a complex global system influenced and shaped by countless socio-economic, political, and technological factors.

The advent of the first department stores represented a turning point in retail history. These were much more than mere shops; they were immersive experiences with spacious areas dedicated to product displays, making shopping a social and cultural experience. People went not just to shop but to experience, to see and be seen.

The diversification of retail formats, with the introduction of supermarkets and discount stores, made consumer goods more accessible and affordable. This marked the beginning of a radical shift in consumer behavior, shifting the focus from quality to quantity and from service to price.

Post-war expansion saw the rise of chains like Walmart, further revolutionizing the sector through aggressive pricing strategies and supply chain optimization. Operational efficiency became the key to success, allowing for cost reduction and increasingly competitive prices. The era of globalization opened new horizons for retail. The opportunity to enter new markets presented both opportunities and challenges. Adapting business models to different cultures and regulations tested the flexibility and innovation of retail giants. In this context, internationalization was not just about geographic expansion but required a deep understanding of local dynamics and careful management of relationships with suppliers and customers.

The digital revolution has opened the door to a new world of possibilities. E-commerce has redefined the rules of the game, breaking down geographical barriers and making shopping an increasingly personalized and on-demand experience. Amazon has led this transformation, harnessing the power of data and technology to offer a wide range of products, fast delivery services, and an unprecedented user experience. But the evolution of retail hasn't stopped at the digital realm. Growing awareness of environmental and social issues has prompted deep reflection on the role of businesses in society. Sustainability has become an imperative, not only to meet consumer demands but also to ensure long-term business resilience and sustainability. Initiatives such as waste recycling, the use of renewable energy, and the promotion of ethical products have gained ground.

The COVID-19 pandemic accelerated many ongoing trends, highlighting the vulnerability of global supply chains and the importance of digitization. The exponential growth of e-commerce during lockdowns emphasized the need for a robust digital infrastructure and efficient logistics solutions. At the same time, it underscored the importance of flexibility and adaptability in an ever-changing world.

Looking to the future, it's clear that retail will continue to evolve, driven by emerging technologies and shifts in consumer behavior. Blockchain, Artificial Intelligence, and the

Internet of Things are just some of the technologies that are already beginning to shape the future of the industry. These offer opportunities to increase efficiency, improve product traceability, and further personalize offerings.

In this dynamic and ever-evolving landscape, retail companies are called upon to navigate uncertain waters, balancing innovation and risk, efficiency and responsibility. The road ahead is filled with challenges, but also opportunities, and it will be interesting to see how they adapt and shape the future of distribution in the modern world.

The transformation of retail can also be seen in the continuous adaptability and reinvention of business strategies and models. Competitive dynamics have become increasingly intense, leading companies to seek unique advantages to stand out in a saturated market. Loyalty programs, product differentiation strategies, and attention to store design are all examples of how retail has sought to attract and retain customers. Another significant dimension is the challenges and opportunities created by ever-evolving consumer expectations. Transparency, authenticity, and integrity have become increasingly important qualities. Modern consumers, armed with digital tools that allow instant price comparison and review checking, have become more demanding and informed. The advent of mass customization has seen retail adopting technologies to analyze consumer data and offer tailor-made products and services. Artificial intelligence and data analysis have enabled the prediction of buying trends and the customization of offerings, creating an increasingly individual-centric shopping experience.

The push toward sustainability and ethics is another crucial aspect. Consumers are increasingly aware of the environmental and social impact of their purchases, and retail companies have responded through the promotion of organic, fair trade, and locally sourced products, as well as the adoption of ethical and sustainable business practices.

The integration of innovative technologies extends beyond e-commerce and data analysis into logistics and inventory management. Warehouse automation and robotics, advanced logistics, and the use of drones and autonomous vehicles for deliveries are all elements shaping the future of retail, reducing delivery times and enhancing operational efficiency.

The importance of relationships with suppliers must also be considered. Large retail chains have developed complex supply and production networks, and managing these relationships is crucial. Price negotiations, quality standards assurance, and risk management are all aspects that influence the success of distribution operations.

Interaction with regulations is another element that cannot be overlooked. Government policies, trade rules, and tax regulations have a significant impact on the structure and operations of retail companies. Compliance is not only a legal requirement but can also influence the company's reputation and image in the eyes of consumers.

Resilience and adaptability have become increasingly important qualities in an era marked by uncertainty and constant change. Economic crises, demographic shifts, evolving consumer trends, and technological advancements are all factors influencing the landscape of retail, necessitating a continuous review and update of strategies and operational models.

The lessons learned from past successes and failures illuminate the path to the future. Case studies and specific analyses offer valuable insights into what works and what doesn't, enabling companies to learn and adapt. The ability to learn and innovate is, therefore, fundamental to maintaining competitiveness in such a dynamic and challenging sector.

In this perspective, the role of human resources and corporate culture is essential. Employee motivation, training, and well-being are key factors that influence productivity and efficiency. Creating a positive and inclusive work environment can be a differentiating factor in the competitive landscape.

Modern retail, therefore, is an ever-evolving sector that reflects and responds to the challenges and opportunities of a rapidly changing world. Its history is a tale of innovation and adaptation, a story that continues to be written every day.

In summary, the history of retail is intricately tied to the fabric of technological, socio-economic, and cultural progress in society. It is characterized by constant evolution, with each era bringing new developments and challenges. From the emergence of the first department stores and supermarkets to the explosion of e-commerce, and to the contemporary emphasis on sustainability and ethics, the sector has witnessed significant transformations that have not only influenced how products are sold and distributed but also the behavior and expectations of consumers.

Technology has played a fundamental role in this evolution, not only through digitization and e-commerce but also through innovations in logistics, automation, and data utilization. These developments have allowed companies to optimize operations, personalize offers, and respond more effectively to consumer needs, but they have also brought new challenges in terms of privacy, security, and competition.

The increasing focus on sustainability and social responsibility represents a significant shift. It's no longer just about offering products at competitive prices but doing so in an ethical and sustainable manner. This paradigm shift is both a response to growing social and environmental concerns and a proactive strategy to build a resilient, long-term business model.

Relationships with suppliers and stakeholders, human resource management, regulatory compliance, and the building of a positive corporate image and reputation are all key elements contributing to success in the modern retail landscape. These factors, along with the ability to quickly adapt to a constantly changing environment, define a company's capacity to remain competitive and thrive.

Finally, the history of retail is a testament to human ingenuity and adaptability. Every challenge has been an opportunity to innovate, every problem has opened the door to new solutions. The intersection of business, technology, and society will continue to shape the future of retail, offering uncharted scenarios and endless possibilities. The ability to learn from the successes and mistakes of the past and navigate this complex and dynamic landscape will determine who emerges as a leader in the retail sector in the future.

2. Types of Retail Structures (Hypermarkets, Supermarkets, Discount Stores, etc.)

In the realm of retail, there are various types of structures that differ in size, product assortment, pricing positioning, and services offered to customers. These include:

1. **Hypermarkets**: Hypermarkets are large retail structures offering a wide range of both food and

non-food products. Characterized by extensive selling areas, they provide a broad selection of merchandise categories, often including clothing, appliances, home goods, and leisure items, in addition to groceries.

2. **Supermarkets**: Supermarkets are smaller in size compared to hypermarkets and primarily focus on the sale of food products, although they also offer a selection of non-food items. They are common in urban and suburban areas and emphasize convenience and proximity to consumers.

3. **Discount Stores**: Discount stores offer products at lower prices compared to other types of retailers. Cost reduction is achieved through a limited product variety, economical packaging, and operational efficiency. These stores attract price-sensitive customers and are often associated with budget brands.

4. **Cash & Carry**: Cash & Carry stores are wholesale warehouses where businesses, and in some cases, consumers, can purchase goods in bulk. These outlets primarily cater to small business owners, retailers, and restaurateurs.

5. **Convenience Stores**: Convenience stores are small shops located in densely populated urban areas or along busy roads. They have extended hours of operation, often open 24/7, and offer a

limited range of everyday products at slightly higher prices than supermarkets.

6. **Specialty Stores**: Specialty stores focus on specific product categories such as electronics, books, or organic products, providing a deep assortment and specialized expertise. They are often characterized by an image of quality and competence in their niche.

7. **Online Retailers**: Online retailers operate on digital platforms, offering a wide range of products that can be purchased over the internet. Amazon is a prominent example of an online retailer. E-commerce has experienced significant growth in recent years, with an increasing number of consumers preferring online shopping for convenience.

8. **Warehouse Clubs**: Warehouse clubs, such as Costco, offer members access to discounted prices on wholesale products in exchange for an annual membership fee. These stores are known for their large size and varied assortment of products.

9. **Pop-up Stores**: Pop-up stores are temporary retail outlets that open for a limited period, often to promote a specific brand or product. They are used as a marketing strategy to create a sense of urgency and exclusivity.

Each of these types of retail structures has unique characteristics and meets different consumer needs. The choice of structure type influences marketing strategy, market positioning, and the consumer shopping experience. Moreover, evolving consumer behavior and technologies continue to shape the retail landscape, giving rise to new formats and business models.

The diversification of retail structure types reflects the changing needs and habits of consumers. Each type of structure is calibrated to address specific requirements, which can vary from a wide product selection to competitive prices to convenience and speed of purchase. For example, while hypermarkets focus on variety and assortment, discount stores concentrate on offering low prices by reducing additional services.

Geographical location is another critical factor in the strategy of these structures. While supermarkets and convenience stores are often situated in central locations or densely populated neighborhoods to attract local consumers, hypermarkets and warehouse clubs can afford to be positioned in more peripheral areas due to their ability to draw customers from a wider geographical area.

Technological advancement has also had a significant impact on the physical shape of stores. The increasing integration of technology in retail, such as mobile apps, self-checkout, and contactless payment systems, has enhanced efficiency and the shopping experience while simultaneously altering store layouts and arrangements.

Store design and atmosphere have become increasingly important elements in the retail strategy. Creating a welcoming environment, using lighting and colors, and organizing space influence consumer shopping behavior and contribute to building the brand image. For instance, specialized stores may use distinctive design elements to communicate their expertise and quality in a particular sector.

Customer loyalty strategies differ significantly among the various types of retail structures. While discount stores may primarily attract customers through low prices, hypermarkets and specialty stores may invest in loyalty programs, personalized services, and unique shopping experiences to build long-term relationships with customers.

Additionally, inventory and logistics management are critical and vary depending on the type of structure. Hypermarkets and warehouse clubs require complex inventory management due to the vast assortment and quantities, while convenience stores and pop-up stores can operate with limited and recurring stock, focusing on high turnover products.

Another relevant aspect is communication and marketing. Each type of structure requires a tailored communication strategy. For example, while online retailers can primarily focus on digital marketing and search engine optimization, supermarkets may still find traditional advertising and in-store promotions effective.

The rise of online commerce has also led to the emergence of new hybrid models. Some supermarket chains are experimenting with click-and-collect models, where customers can order online and pick up in-store, combining the convenience of online shopping with the speed of on-site pickup.

The increasing importance of sustainability is influencing the operational strategies of all types of structures. The adoption of eco-friendly practices, such as the use of sustainable packaging, waste reduction, and the offering of local and organic products, is becoming a distinctive element and added value for consumers.

In this dynamic context, the ability to anticipate trends, adapt to market changes, and continuously innovate is essential to remain competitive and meet consumers' increasingly high expectations in terms of quality, price, service, and responsibility. A deep understanding of the specific characteristics and dynamics of each type of structure is fundamental for developing effective and sustainable strategies over time.

Furthermore, as we analyze the variety of structures in retail, it is essential to highlight how personalized offerings and differentiation have become key strategies. The increasing diversity in consumer needs and purchasing behaviors requires an increasingly segmented and targeted approach. For example, some supermarkets are expanding their offering of organic, local, and niche products to attract quality and origin-conscious customers.

Operational flexibility is another essential element. Structures must be able to adapt quickly to changes in consumer behavior, market conditions, and regulations. The introduction of advanced technologies, such as robotics and artificial intelligence, is transforming inventory management, logistics, and customer interactions, making operations more efficient and responsive.

It is also interesting to note the evolution of relationships between manufacturers and retailers. Power dynamics and collaboration models are continually evolving, with increasing supply chain integration and the emergence of strategic partnerships. Transparency and traceability of raw materials and finished products have become central issues, fueling the growing demand for certifications and quality standards.

At the same time, corporate social responsibility is playing an increasingly central role in the retail strategy. Attention to environmental sustainability, workers' rights, and the well-being of local communities has become crucial in brand perception and consumer loyalty. In this context, corporate social responsibility initiatives and ethical business practices are essential tools for building a positive image and attracting socially conscious customers.

Price and promotional strategies vary greatly among different types of structures. While discount stores and warehouse clubs mainly compete on price, offering low-cost products in a no-frills environment, specialty stores and luxury shops focus on creating an exclusive shopping experience and offering high-quality products and premium services. Defining the right pricing strategy requires a deep understanding of the market, competitors, and customer expectations and can have a significant impact on the profitability of the business.

In the omnichannel context, the integration between physical and digital channels is crucial. Online presence has become essential for brand visibility and customer attraction, while physical stores continue to play a crucial role in providing personalized service and building customer relationships. Combining online and offline channels allows reaching a broader audience and offering a variety of ways to interact with the brand, increasing sales and loyalty opportunities.

Finally, the training and development of personnel are crucial aspects for the success of the retail industry. The quality of customer service, competence, and professionalism of employees can make a difference in a competitive market. Investing in employee training and well-being is, therefore, a winning strategy to improve customer satisfaction and company performance.

Looking at the entire landscape, it is clear that modern retail is a complex and dynamic sector in which the ability to innovate, adapt, and respond to consumer needs is fundamental for long-term success.

In summary, the variety and complexity of the types of structures in modern retail are representative of the adaptation and innovation that characterize this industry. From the size and geographical location of hypermarkets to the pricing models of discount stores, each type of structure reveals a strategy tailored to meet specific consumer needs.

Ongoing technological evolution has made greater operational efficiency possible and has transformed the way customers interact with retail structures, giving rise to new business models and hybrid solutions between physical and digital. Environmental sustainability and corporate social responsibility have become central priorities, influencing not only daily operations but also brand image and consumer relationships.

The relationships between manufacturers and distributors have undergone significant transformations, with the establishment of new power dynamics and collaboration, fueling the need for greater transparency and traceability. Price and promotional strategies, diversified and tailored to the characteristics of each type of structure, reflect the importance of a deep understanding of the market and customer expectations.

The integration of physical and digital channels has become an essential component of sales strategies, allowing reaching a broader audience and offering a variety of ways to interact with the brand. And finally, the focus on human capital, training, and personnel development emphasizes the crucial role that employee competence and professionalism play in the success of retail structures.

Through a detailed understanding of these dynamics, it is possible to appreciate the complexity and richness of the modern retail sector and identify strategic levers to compete successfully in an ever-evolving market. Modern retail, therefore, represents a microcosm where innovation, adaptation, sustainability, and human relationships meet and intertwine, constituting a fundamental element of the

contemporary economy and the daily lives of
people.

3. Geography of Distribution (Location, Concentration, etc.)

The geography of distribution is a crucial element
in the strategy of large retail chains. The location,
concentration, and geographical arrangement of
retail outlets directly impact a company's success
and competitiveness in the industry.

1. Location:

- **Urban Centers:** Many supermarkets and
convenience stores are located in urban centers
or city outskirts to reach a dense population.
Proximity to customers is essential for foot traffic
and purchase frequency.
- **Peripheral Areas:** Hypermarkets and
shopping centers are often situated in the
outskirts, where ample space and parking are
available, attracting a broader customer base.

- **Rural Areas:** In these areas, you can find small convenience stores or proximity supermarkets serving less densely populated communities.

2. Concentration and Competition:

- **High Concentration:** In some geographical areas, the presence of numerous retail outlets from different brands can intensify competition, influencing pricing and assortment strategies.
- **Monopoly/Duopoly:** In some regions or cities, the presence of a single major player or two primary competitors can determine specific market dynamics.

3. Accessibility and Infrastructure:

- **Transportation Routes:** Proximity to major roads, highways, and public transportation infrastructure is essential for visibility and accessibility.
- **Parking and Services:** The availability of parking and additional services such as banks, pharmacies, and dining enhances attractiveness.

4. Demographics and Territory Characteristics:

- **Population:** Demographic analysis, population density, and purchasing power influence location choice and store type.

- **Socioeconomic Characteristics:** The consumption habits, preferences, and needs of the local population must be analyzed to optimize the offering.

5. Environmental and Regulatory Factors:

- **Local Regulations:** Local regulations and ordinances related to construction, the environment, and commerce can influence store location and operation.
- **Sustainability:** Environmental impact and sustainability play an increasing role in location and construction decisions.

6. Trends and Future Developments:

- **E-commerce and Logistics:** The growth of e-commerce affects distribution geography, necessitating strategic warehouses and distribution centers.
- **Urbanization and Mobility:** Urbanization trends and changes in urban mobility can bring new opportunities and challenges to store location.
-
  Thoroughly analyzing the geography of distribution and adopting an optimal location strategy is essential to maximize market coverage, attract the right customer base, and compete effectively in the retail landscape.

Furthermore, when further analyzing the geography of distribution, it's evident that the influence of location extends beyond mere physical proximity to consumers. For example, the choice of location can significantly impact branding and a company's image. Being present in prestigious locations or high-traffic areas can enhance brand visibility and perception, while being present in demographically diverse areas can help reach different market segments. Additionally, the internal store layout and architectural design can be influenced by local geography. Space availability, terrain characteristics, and the specifics of urban or rural contexts can determine design and operational decisions, affecting the customer shopping experience and operational efficiency. Location strategy isn't just about the choice of place but also the timing. Market trends, economic fluctuations, and demographic changes can make some areas more or less attractive over time. Temporal analysis and adaptation to market dynamics are therefore crucial to maintaining relevance and competitiveness. Managing relationships with the local community is another crucial aspect. Community acceptance and support can facilitate market entry and contribute to long-term success. Conversely, community resistance and opposition to new openings can pose significant obstacles. Participation in local initiatives, creating partnerships, and listening to the community's needs are key strategies in this context.

Integration with other commercial actors and services can also influence location strategy. The presence of other stores, restaurants, services, and attractions nearby can increase the attractiveness of the location and generate synergies. Integration with the local commercial and social fabric can create opportunities for collaboration and joint marketing.
The geography of distribution is closely linked to logistics and the supply chain. Proximity to suppliers, distribution centers, and transport hubs is crucial to optimize transportation costs and ensure product freshness and availability. In this regard, digitization and technological innovation are bringing significant changes, with the introduction of sustainable transportation solutions, intelligent logistics platforms, and advanced traceability systems.

Finally, the geography of distribution is also influenced by changes in consumer behavior and evolving purchasing habits. The increasing interest in online commerce, a focus on sustainability and local production, and the pursuit of unique and personalized shopping experiences are shaping the landscape of retail and influencing localization and development strategies.

In this dynamic and multifactorial context, the ability to interpret and anticipate trends, adapt to the local environment, and integrate with the community and local economic fabric are key competencies for modern retail.

Digging deeper, it's evident that another essential element in the geography of distribution is the detailed analysis of the socio-cultural context of an area. Local culture, traditions, values, and social norms significantly influence consumption habits and can determine the success or failure of a retail outlet. Understanding and respecting the local culture is, therefore, fundamental to developing an offering and service that meets the needs and expectations of the community.

Furthermore, the political and institutional dimension of the settlement area plays a significant role. Local, regional, and national policies, urban regulations, incentives, and constraints can either facilitate or complicate the opening and management of retail locations. A good relationship with local authorities and a deep understanding of the regulatory framework are essential to successfully navigate the institutional context.

Another relevant aspect is the resilience and flexibility of the distribution network. Retail companies must be able to quickly adapt to sudden changes in the environment, such as economic crises, extreme weather events, or health emergencies. The ability to maintain operational continuity and respond effectively to crisis scenarios is, therefore, a key element of distribution strategy.

Technology and digitalization are also strategic tools for optimizing the geography of distribution. Advanced use of data and analytics allows for refining location choices, improving inventory management, customizing offerings, and enhancing customer interaction. Technological innovation offers new opportunities to make the distribution network more effective and sustainable.

In the context of sustainability, assessing the environmental impact of distribution activities is increasingly central. Choices related to materials, energy efficiency of buildings, waste and emissions management, and the promotion of sustainable and local products all influence the reputation and long-term performance of a business.

Finally, the evolution of competitive dynamics leads retail companies to explore new geographic frontiers. Internationalization and expansion into new markets are ambitious strategies that require a deep understanding of local specifics and a strong capacity for adaptation. The challenges and opportunities of international markets add an additional layer of complexity to the geography of distribution.

In this diverse and ever-evolving landscape, modern retail must balance its connection to the local community with innovation and respond to local needs while maintaining a global vision. Only through a strategic and informed approach can retail businesses create distribution networks that are simultaneously resilient, sustainable, and competitive, capable of meeting the demands of an increasingly discerning and evolving market.

4. Technological Evolution (E-commerce, Apps, Self-Checkout, etc.)

Technological evolution has had a profound and transformative impact on the retail industry, altering both consumer interactions and internal operations. This evolution is evident in various aspects, including the rise of e-commerce, the development of mobile applications, the introduction of self-checkout systems, and much more.

E-commerce has revolutionized how consumers purchase products, offering convenience, extensive choices, and competitive prices. Retail has had to adapt to this new reality by developing online platforms, optimizing logistics, and integrating physical and digital channels. Online shopping experiences have become increasingly personalized, thanks to the use of big data and artificial intelligence, which analyze user preferences and offer tailored products and deals.

Mobile applications have become essential tools for connecting consumers with retail outlets. Through apps, customers can access personalized discounts, locate the nearest stores, check product availability, and more. These applications also collect valuable data on purchasing behavior, enhancing customer insights and refining marketing strategies.

Self-checkout represents another significant innovation, allowing customers to independently pay for their items, reducing wait times, and improving store operational efficiency. This technological solution has also driven the development of advanced anti-fraud and security systems.

Other technological developments include the integration of **robotics and automation** in logistics and warehouse processes, the use of **RFID labels** for product traceability, and the application of **augmented and virtual reality** to enhance the shopping experience.

Sustainability has become a key factor, driving the adoption of eco-friendly technological solutions such as LED lighting, energy management systems, and recyclable or biodegradable materials.

Finally, technological evolution has led to the creation of new business models and partnerships, including collaborations between retailers and technology startups, the expansion into local product markets through digital platforms, and the development of integrated service ecosystems. The entire retail landscape has been shaped and continuously reshaped by these technological advancements, introducing new possibilities, challenges, and opportunities. The ability to adapt quickly and make the most of the potential offered by technology has become a distinctive and competitive element for businesses in the industry.

In parallel with the rise of e-commerce and apps, blockchain technologies are finding applications in the retail sector. This technology allows for tracking the origin and movement of products along the supply chain, increasing transparency and consumer trust. Blockchain has the potential to revolutionize supply chain management, reducing the risk of fraud and counterfeiting, and enhancing corporate social responsibility.

Virtual Reality (VR) and Augmented Reality (AR) are transforming the retail shopping experience. These technologies offer customers the ability to visualize products in a three-dimensional environment, virtually try on clothing and accessories, or access additional information about items using mobile devices. This type of interaction enhances customer engagement and can positively influence purchasing decisions.

The growing importance of **Artificial Intelligence (AI) and Machine Learning (ML)** is another unstoppable trend in the industry. These technologies enable the analysis of vast amounts of data to predict buying behaviors, optimize inventory, personalize offers, and improve operational efficiency. AI also underlies the development of chatbots and virtual assistants that can guide customers during their shopping and provide real-time responses to their questions and needs.

The increasing use of **drones for product delivery** represents an innovative solution to reduce delivery times and reach remote or hard-to-access areas. While this technology is still in development and regulation, it could become a key element in retail distribution logistics.

The proliferation of wearable devices and Internet of Things (IoT)-connected objects offers new possibilities for data collection and customer interaction. Devices such as smartwatches and fitness trackers can provide insights into consumer habits and preferences, enabling companies to offer increasingly personalized services and products.

Sustainability and Eco-Friendly Packaging
In the realm of environmental sustainability, the research and development of eco-friendly packaging and waste reduction solutions are gaining prominence. Technologies like 3D printing can contribute to the creation of customized packaging, reducing material usage and minimizing waste.

Furthermore, the advent of **5G technology** is accelerating the digitalization of retail, enhancing connectivity and enabling the development of innovative services and applications. The increased speed and data transmission capacity open the door to immersive shopping experiences, fast and secure payment solutions, and greater integration between physical and digital channels.

Lastly, innovation in payment systems, with the emergence of solutions such as contactless payments, digital wallets, and cryptocurrencies, is reshaping economic transactions within the retail industry, offering consumers more choices, convenience, and security.

Personalization Driven by Technology

The drive toward personalization, powered by new technologies, is giving rise to increasingly tailored shopping experiences. Recommendation algorithms, based on machine learning, analyze user purchase and browsing data, suggesting products and offers aligned with their interests and past behaviors, thereby improving customer conversion and loyalty.

Emerging Biometric Technology

Biometrics is another emerging technology in the retail sector. Facial recognition and fingerprint scanning are used to expedite transactions, enhance security, and provide a more personalized service. This technology is finding applications not only in payment systems but also in access management and store security.

Voice-Commerce Technology Adoption

Another significant trend is the adoption of voice-commerce technology. Intelligent voice assistants like Alexa, Google Assistant, and Siri are becoming increasingly popular, with consumers starting to use them for product searches, price comparisons, and completing purchases. This changes how consumers interact with e-commerce platforms and requires companies to optimize their content for voice search.

Gamification for Customer Engagement

Gamification, which involves incorporating game elements into non-gaming contexts, is becoming an effective tool for engaging and motivating consumers. Loyalty programs, challenges, and virtual rewards are used to increase customer retention, encourage repeat purchases, and gather valuable feedback and data.

Predictive Analysis with Machine Learning

Predictive analysis, based on machine learning techniques, is used to anticipate market trends, predict the demand for specific products, and optimize inventory management. This allows companies to reduce waste, improve efficiency, and enhance customer satisfaction.

Ethical Considerations in Technology

In the context of retail, technology ethics has become a crucial issue. Matters concerning data privacy, information security, and the ethical use of artificial intelligence are at the forefront of the debate. Companies are called upon to operate responsibly, ensuring transparency and respect for consumer rights.

Smart Cities and Urban Ecosystems

Smart cities, where technology is used to enhance quality of life and service efficiency, offer new opportunities for the retail industry. Increasing connectivity and interaction between various sectors, such as transportation, energy, and retail, enable the creation of integrated urban ecosystems, where access to goods and services is facilitated and optimized.

Mixed Reality in Retail

Mixed reality, which combines elements of augmented and virtual reality, is beginning to make its appearance in the retail sector. This technology enables the creation of immersive and interactive experiences in which users can view products in a three-dimensional environment, modify item characteristics, and access real-time additional information.

Finally, the growing importance of the circular economy is a factor that retail companies cannot ignore. The need to reduce environmental impact is driving businesses to rethink their business models, promote reuse, recycling, and sustainability, and adopt technologies that support these practices.

The implementation of data-driven distribution networks is leading to a profound optimization of operations. Data analysis enables companies to monitor the movement of goods in real-time, predict delivery times more accurately, and proactively respond to any unforeseen circumstances. This contributes to reducing operational costs and improving customer satisfaction.

Another rapidly evolving field is robotics. Robots are becoming increasingly common in warehouses and distribution centers, where they perform tasks such as packaging, transporting goods, and managing inventory. Robotic process automation is enhancing efficiency, reducing human errors, and enabling quick adaptation to demand fluctuations.

The growing interest in renewable energy and sustainability is also influencing the retail industry. Companies are investing in sustainable energy solutions such as solar panels and wind turbines to power their facilities and reduce carbon footprints. The goal is to contribute to the fight against climate change and meet the growing consumer expectations regarding sustainability.

Furthermore, the Internet of Things (IoT) is having a significant impact on supply chain management. Sensors and connected devices allow real-time monitoring of product storage conditions, precise location tracking of goods, and timely detection of anomalies. This leads to increased transparency, waste reduction, and better resource management.

The retail industry is also exploring the possibilities offered by 3D printing. This technology can be used to produce spare parts on demand, customize products according to customer needs, and reduce production times. 3D printing could revolutionize production and distribution models, bringing production closer to the point of sale and reducing the need for warehouses.

Digital payment technologies continue to evolve, offering increasingly innovative and secure solutions. Contactless payment technologies such as Near Field Communication (NFC) enable fast and secure transactions, reducing checkout times and enhancing the shopping experience.

Additionally, the growing interest in health and wellness is influencing the variety and types of products offered by the retail industry. Companies are responding to the demand for organic, gluten-free, vegan, and low-sugar products, adapting their offerings, and experimenting with new formats and sales channels.

Another factor shaping the industry is the rise of ethical and sustainable brands. Consumers are becoming increasingly aware of the environmental and social impact of their purchases and seek products that align with their values. This is prompting companies to rethink their strategies, invest in sustainable production practices, and transparently communicate their ethical commitments.

Collaborations between technology companies and retailers are becoming more common to develop innovative solutions and address market challenges. These partnerships can lead to new business opportunities, skill enhancement, and the creation of added value for customers.

Finally, the increasing globalization of the market is leading to greater competition but also new opportunities for international expansion. Retail companies must adapt to different cultural, regulatory, and market contexts by developing flexible and sustainable strategies to succeed on a global scale.

Technological Evolution in Retail: Shaping the Future

Technological evolution in the retail industry has led to an unprecedented transformation, introducing and implementing numerous technological innovations, each of which has contributed to shaping and influencing the entire ecosystem.

E-commerce, Mobile Apps, and Self-Checkout Systems

The adoption of technologies like e-commerce, mobile apps, and self-checkout systems has not only provided consumers with more options and convenience in their shopping but has also helped retailers gather valuable data, optimize store and warehouse operations, and personalize offerings based on customer preferences. E-commerce, in particular, has allowed retailers to reach a global audience, transcending geographical barriers and creating new market opportunities.

Artificial Intelligence and Machine Learning

Artificial intelligence and machine learning play a pivotal role in consumer data analysis, trend forecasting, and offer personalization. These technological tools enable advanced customer segmentation, a better understanding of consumer needs and desires, and a more effective response to market demands.

Biometric and Facial Recognition Technologies

Biometric and facial recognition technologies have been implemented to enhance security and expedite transactions, while voice assistants are changing how consumers search for and purchase products, making voice search an essential element of digital marketing strategies.

Gamification and Predictive Analysis

Gamification is used to increase customer engagement, and predictive analysis contributes to optimizing inventory management and waste prevention. Additionally, a focus on sustainability and ethics is influencing business decisions, with a growing adoption of circular economy practices and a commitment to transparency and responsibility.

Innovations in IoT, Robotics, and 3D Printing

Innovations in the Internet of Things (IoT), robotics, and 3D printing are bringing significant improvements in operational efficiency, supply chain management, and product customization. 3D printing, in particular, offers revolutionary possibilities, bringing production closer to the

point of sale and reducing the need for
warehouses.

Digital Payment Technologies

The introduction and evolution of digital
payment technologies are enhancing the
shopping experience, making transactions faster
and more secure, while the increasing variety of
products meets consumers' new health and
wellness needs.

**Tech Company-Retailer Collaborations
and Globalization**

Collaborations between technology companies
and retailers, along with market globalization,
are creating an increasingly competitive,
dynamic, and diversified retail landscape. The
ability to adapt quickly to new technologies and
trends, respond ethically and sustainably to
consumer needs, and navigate successfully in an
international context will be key elements for the
future of retail.

In summary, technological evolution is
profoundly influencing every aspect of retail,
from production to distribution, from marketing
to sales, and continues to offer new opportunities
and challenges for retailers and consumers alike.
Understanding and adopting these technologies
are essential for those operating in this industry
and aiming to remain competitive in an ever-
evolving market.

5. Logistics and Supply Chain

Logistics and the supply chain are fundamental elements in the retail industry. They encompass all the processes and activities required to transport products from their point of origin to the point of sale while efficiently managing inventory and meeting consumer demand.

1. **Efficiency and Optimization:** The need to reduce costs and delivery times has led to a constant quest for efficiency and optimization. The adoption of advanced information systems, such as Enterprise Resource Planning (ERP) and Warehouse Management Systems (WMS), allows for more accurate inventory management, real-time shipment tracking, and optimized transportation planning.
2. **Sustainability:** Growing environmental concerns are driving companies to seek sustainable logistics solutions. This includes the use of low-impact vehicles, reduced packaging, transportation route optimization to minimize CO_2 emissions, and the adoption of circular economy practices.
3. **Technological Innovation:** The implementation of new technologies is revolutionizing logistics. Innovations such as RFID tracking systems, warehouse robotics,

drones for deliveries, and big data analytics are improving the efficiency and speed of the supply chain.

4. **Globalization:** Retail operates in a global market, and supply chain management must consider challenges related to market diversity, local regulations, cultural differences, and currency fluctuations.

5. **Demand Response:** Companies must be able to adapt quickly to changes in consumer demand. This requires precise planning, high flexibility, and rapid responsiveness. Predictive analysis and forecasting techniques are essential tools for predicting market trends and adjusting production and distribution accordingly.

6. **E-commerce:** The explosion of e-commerce has brought about new logistics challenges, such as managing direct-to-consumer deliveries, returns, and service personalization. Companies are exploring solutions like delivery lockers, pickup points, and urban logistics to meet online customers' expectations.

7. **Risks and Crisis Management:** The supply chain is exposed to various risks, including disruptions, delays, fluctuations in raw material prices, and natural disasters. Companies must implement risk management strategies and contingency plans to minimize the impact of such events.

8. **Supplier Relationships:** Managing relationships with suppliers is crucial to ensuring product quality, a continuous supply, and favorable contract negotiations. Companies are adopting collaborative approaches and digital platforms to improve communication and transparency with supply chain partners.

9. **Customization and Personalization:** The trend toward product customization and personalization requires more flexible and responsive logistics capable of handling small batches and a variety of Stock Keeping Units (SKUs).

10. **Training and Workforce Development:** Workforce training is essential to maintaining high standards of safety and efficiency in logistics operations. Companies invest in skills development programs and ongoing training to ensure the readiness of their employees.

In summary, logistics and the supply chain in the retail sector are constantly evolving, influenced by external factors such as technology, globalization, and consumer expectations. Adapting to these dynamics and adopting innovative solutions are essential for the competitiveness and success of companies in the industry.

Logistics and Supply Chain in Retail: Emerging Trends

Logistics and the supply chain in the retail sector are vital areas that employ a variety of strategies and technologies to ensure products reach consumers in the most efficient and effective manner. In this regard, it's essential to explore further aspects and emerging trends shaping these domains.

1. **Integration of Digital Technologies:** Beyond RFID systems and drones, technologies like blockchain are finding applications in product traceability along the supply chain. This technology offers greater transparency, reduces the risk of fraud, and enhances contract management among supply chain stakeholders.

2. **Automation and Robotics:** Automation continues to play a central role in warehouses, with robots collecting, packaging, and moving goods, reducing execution time and minimizing errors. The use of autonomous vehicles in freight transport is also growing, offering potential improvements in safety and efficiency.

3. **Data Analytics and Artificial Intelligence:** The implementation of advanced data analytics algorithms and artificial intelligence enables companies to optimize transportation routes, predict delivery times with greater accuracy, and

anticipate potential supply chain issues, allowing for proactive interventions.

4. **Omnichannel:** The increasing demand for omnichannel shopping experiences by consumers is driving retailers to integrate physical and digital channels, creating logistic challenges in terms of inventory management, delivery times, and after-sales services.

5. **Micro-Fulfillment Centers:** To reduce delivery times and bring inventory closer to consumers, new models like micro-fulfillment centers are emerging. These small distribution centers are located in densely populated urban areas to facilitate the rapid delivery of products ordered online.

6. **Circular Economy and Reuse:** The integration of circular economy practices into logistics is becoming increasingly important. Reusing packaging and pallets, as well as recycling and recovering materials, are key strategies for reducing the environmental impact of logistics operations.

7. **Last-Mile Delivery:** Last-mile delivery is one of the most complex and costly segments of the supply chain, especially in urban areas. Solutions range from crowdsourcing, using independent couriers for deliveries, to exploring innovative models like refrigerated lockers for food products.

8. **Regulations and Compliance:** Retail companies must navigate a sea of regulations and standards that vary from country to country. Compliance with these regulations is crucial to avoid penalties and ensure a positive market reputation.

9. **Relationship Management:** The relationship between retailers and suppliers is becoming increasingly collaborative. The adoption of digital platforms facilitates information sharing and promotes greater transparency and cooperation in addressing common challenges.

10. **Service Customization:** The ability to offer personalized logistics services is increasingly important to meet the diverse needs of consumers. This includes flexible delivery options, real-time order tracking, and efficient after-sales services.

These trends and developments underscore the complexity and dynamism of the logistics sector in retail, highlighting the importance of innovative strategies and advanced technological solutions to maintain competitiveness in a rapidly evolving market.

Logistics and the supply chain continue to evolve, incorporating new challenges and opportunities in the realm of retail. Let's explore further dynamics and prospects that characterize this industry.

Inventory Management Strategies

Inventory management is a vital element as maintaining the right balance between supply and demand is crucial to reduce costs and prevent product shortages. Techniques such as Just-In-Time and real-time sales data analysis are fundamental for maintaining optimal inventory levels.

Impact of the Pandemic

The COVID-19 pandemic has stress-tested the global supply chain, highlighting vulnerabilities and the need for greater resilience. Strategies such as supplier diversification, regionalization of supply chains, and investment in digital technologies are being adopted to mitigate future risks.

Reverse Logistics

Reverse logistics, which involves operations related to product returns, is a growing area, especially in e-commerce. Efficient management of returns is crucial for maintaining customer satisfaction and minimizing associated costs.

Cybersecurity

With the increasing digitalization, protecting data and information systems has become a priority. Companies are investing in advanced cybersecurity solutions to safeguard sensitive information and prevent disruptions in logistics operations.

Standardization and Interoperability

Standardizing processes and promoting interoperability among different information systems used along the supply chain are essential to ensure smooth and efficient logistics operations.

Multilateral Collaboration

Collaborative approaches among various supply chain stakeholders, including companies, suppliers, and port authorities, are essential to optimize the entire logistics network and address challenges such as port congestion and customs regulations.

Product Customization

The rising demand for personalized products has implications for logistics, requiring increased flexibility in production and distribution and the ability to manage a wider variety of SKUs (Stock Keeping Units).

Packaging Innovations

Innovations in packaging, including the use of sustainable materials and solutions to reduce packaging volume, are a trend that influences logistics, contributing to reduced transportation costs and environmental impact.

Skills Development

The evolving sector necessitates continuous training for logistics and supply chain professionals to develop skills in digital, analytical, and relationship management areas.

Infrastructure Development

Investment in logistics infrastructure, such as warehouses, distribution hubs, and transportation networks, is crucial to support business expansion and ensure operational efficiency.

These additional dynamics demonstrate the complexity and multidimensionality of the logistics and supply chain field in the retail industry, underscoring the need for an integrated and innovative approach to successfully navigate this ever-evolving environment.

Environmental Sustainability

The concept of sustainability is gaining traction in logistics. Companies are driven, both by regulations and increasing consumer awareness, to reduce their environmental impact. This translates into initiatives to reduce CO_2 emissions, the use of electric vehicles for distribution, and the adoption of circular economy solutions throughout the supply chain.

Global Market Dynamics

The supply chain landscape is also heavily influenced by global market dynamics, such as currency fluctuations, trade conflicts, and political uncertainties. Companies must, therefore, develop adaptive strategies and operational resilience to effectively respond to these challenges.

Predictive Artificial Intelligence

Advancements in artificial intelligence technologies enable predictive analysis, allowing companies to anticipate consumer demand, optimize inventory levels, and prevent production and distribution bottlenecks, thus ensuring operational continuity.

Ethics and Social Responsibility

Ethics and social responsibility have become pillars in supply chain management. Respect for human rights, fair working conditions, and the fight against corruption are key elements that retail companies are integrating into their policies and operational practices.

Internet of Things (IoT)

The Internet of Things continues to revolutionize logistics. Connected sensors and devices allow real-time monitoring of transport conditions, precise cargo tracking, and the collection of valuable data to optimize operations and reduce costs.

Cloud Solutions

Cloud solutions are becoming the standard for data management in the supply chain. Offering scalability, accessibility, and security, the cloud enables greater collaboration among different supply chain actors and facilitates the implementation of innovative solutions.

Personalization of Logistics Services

Consumer expectations for increasingly personalized services are driving an evolution in logistics offerings. Options such as scheduled delivery, flexible pickup points, and tailored post-sales services are in high demand and integrated by retailers.

Scenario Analysis and Strategic Planning

The importance of scenario analysis and strategic planning is on the rise. Companies are adopting advanced forecasting models and adaptive strategies to navigate increasingly volatile and competitive markets, ensuring both efficiency and sustainability.

Resilience and Risk Management

Creating resilient supply chains and proactive risk management have become top priorities. Companies are developing business continuity plans, diversifying suppliers and distribution channels, and implementing advanced technologies to monitor and respond to potential risks.

Innovation and Research and Development

Investment in innovation and research and development is crucial for maintaining competitiveness. Companies are exploring new technological solutions, operational models, and strategic partnerships to improve supply chain performance and create added value.

These additional insights outline the breadth and depth of developments and challenges in the field of logistics and supply chain in the retail industry, underscoring the importance of a holistic and proactive approach to meet the growing demands of an ever-evolving sector.

Robotization and Automation

The advent of robotic and automated solutions is transforming warehouse and distribution operations. Autonomous robots, automated shelving systems, and drones are employed to optimize picking, packing, and delivery activities, reducing transit times and minimizing human errors.

Blockchain for Traceability

Blockchain technology is emerging as a fundamental tool to ensure traceability and transparency throughout the entire supply chain. It securely and immutably records all transactions, facilitating product origin certification and quality certification management.

Omnichannel Integration

Omnichannel integration is crucial in an increasingly digitally-oriented retail context.

Companies are striving to synergistically connect online and offline channels, ensuring a consistent shopping experience and efficient inventory management across different retail points and e-commerce platforms.

Big Data Analytics
The use of Big Data Analytics is revolutionizing how companies analyze and interpret data. It allows processing large volumes of data from various sources, generating valuable insights to optimize demand, improve operational efficiency, and personalize consumer offerings.

Renewable Energy and Energy Efficiency
The adoption of renewable energy solutions and the implementation of energy efficiency practices in distribution centers and transportation are essential to reduce the carbon footprint of logistics operations and meet environmental sustainability goals.

Development of Logistic Ecosystems
Building integrated logistic ecosystems is becoming a key practice. These ecosystems involve suppliers, manufacturers, distributors, and retailers collaborating through digital platforms to synchronize operations, share information, and create synergies.

International Legislation and Regulations
Compliance with international legislation and regulations is crucial, especially for companies

operating on a global scale. Tariffs, environmental regulations, safety standards, and other legal considerations influence logistics and supply chain operations.

Health and Workplace Safety

Worker health and safety management is a top priority. Implementing safe practices, adequately training personnel, and ensuring optimal working conditions are essential elements in preventing accidents and maintaining high levels of productivity.

Community Engagement

Retail companies are increasingly seeking to establish positive relationships with local communities. This includes adopting ethical and sustainable practices, engaging in community activities, and collaborating with local authorities.

Demographic Dynamics and Consumer Preferences

Demographic dynamics and the evolution of consumer preferences have a significant impact on the supply chain. Analyzing these trends is crucial for predicting changes in demand and adjusting the offering of products and services. Every aspect just explored contributes to the complexity and continuous evolution of the logistics and supply chain sector in retail, requiring a constant commitment to innovation and adaptation to new challenges and opportunities.

Personalization and Micro-Segmentation

The growing demand for personalization and the ability to micro-segment markets based on consumer behavioral data have a significant impact. The ability to create tailored offerings requires flexibility and responsiveness in the supply chain to quickly meet evolving needs and desires.

Circular Economy and Upcycling

Interest in the circular economy and upcycling is intensifying. Companies are exploring innovative ways to reuse, recycle, and add value to products and materials, contributing to waste reduction and promoting environmental sustainability.

Last-Mile Delivery

Last-mile delivery is one of the primary points of differentiation and competition. Creative solutions such as pickup lockers, same-day deliveries, and drones are being implemented to improve efficiency and customer satisfaction.

Multichannel and Cross-Channel Strategies

Multichannel and cross-channel strategies are essential in a market where consumers use various channels to interact with brands. Ensuring consistency, smoothness, and integration across different channels is crucial for delivering an optimal shopping experience.

Cybersecurity

With digitalization, cybersecurity has become a priority. Protecting customer data, transactions, and business operations is essential to prevent cyberattacks, fraud, and the loss of sensitive information.

Gamification and Customer Engagement

The introduction of gamification elements in apps and digital platforms is used to increase customer engagement. This influences inventory management and promotion planning based on customer participation and interaction.

Impact of Social Media

Social media play an increasingly decisive role in shaping consumer preferences. Online reviews, influencers, and digital marketing campaigns influence brand perception and, consequently, product demand.

Expansion into New Markets

Expansion into new geographical markets or market segments represents both an opportunity and a challenge. It requires a deep understanding of local dynamics, customization of offerings, and the creation of efficient distribution networks.

Crisis and Contingency Scenarios

Planning for crisis scenarios and developing contingency plans is essential. Unexpected events such as pandemics, natural disasters, or economic crises can disrupt the supply chain, necessitating the ability to adapt and respond promptly.

Partnering and Strategic Alliances

Forming partnerships and strategic alliances with other industry players, innovative startups, or technology providers can contribute to enhancing the competitiveness, innovation, and efficiency of the supply chain.

Education and Workforce Training

Investing in the education and training of the workforce is essential to maintain high levels of competence, efficiency, and adaptability to technological and market changes.

Analyzing these additional aspects, it becomes evident how logistics and supply chain management in the retail industry are influenced by a multitude of factors and trends, necessitating a holistic view and a continuous process of updating and adaptation.

In summary, logistics and supply chain management in the retail industry are inherently dynamic and multifaceted fields that require the implementation of advanced strategies and continuous adaptation to a rapidly evolving environment. Key concepts such as robotics, blockchain, omnichannel integration, Big Data analytics, energy efficiency, and the creation of integrated logistics ecosystems represent only a few of the fundamental elements driving the transformation of the sector. These aspects, coupled with sustainability initiatives like the circular economy and upcycling, outline a landscape where technological innovation and environmental and social responsibility are increasingly intertwined.

Furthermore, the growing importance of a holistic and integrated customer experience has led to the development of advanced multichannel and cross-channel strategies aimed at creating a seamless and consistent shopping experience across all sales channels. Customer-centricity is also reflected in the evolution of delivery practices, with the emergence of creative solutions for last-mile delivery and increased engagement through gamification techniques.

At the same time, the need to ensure information security has made cybersecurity an indispensable pillar of operations, while the increasing role of social media and online reviews highlights how brand reputation can be significantly influenced by public perception.

Expanding into new markets and market segments, forming strategic partnerships, and investing in workforce education and training are additional strategic levers. These enable navigating the challenges of the global context, enhancing competitiveness, and responding promptly to crisis scenarios and contingencies. Finally, the holistic and multidimensional perspective characterizing modern logistics and supply chain management underscores the importance of an integrated view that takes into account the interconnections among various factors and trends. In this landscape, the ability to analyze, interpret, and anticipate market dynamics and technological developments becomes fundamental to ensuring the sustainability, efficiency, and long-term success of operations in the retail industry.

6. Inventory and Warehouse Management

Inventory and warehouse management are crucial components of modern retail, aiming to optimize inventory levels, reduce costs, and enhance customer satisfaction. This domain encompasses various practices, technologies, and strategies that contribute to ensuring product availability while minimizing the risk of overcapacity or shortages.

Tracking Technologies and RFID

Tracking technologies such as barcodes and RFID tags are essential for monitoring the movement of goods within the warehouse and throughout the supply chain. These technologies enable efficient inventory management and reduce errors.

Warehouse Management System (WMS)

WMS systems are software designed to optimize warehouse operations. They handle receiving, storage, order preparation, and shipping, improving efficiency and reducing lead times.

Just In Time and Lean Inventory

The concept of Just In Time involves receiving goods only when needed, thus reducing stock levels and freeing up warehouse space. Lean Inventory is a similar strategy focused on waste reduction and resource optimization.

Demand Forecasting and Data Analysis

Using data analysis tools and demand forecasting algorithms is essential for predicting market fluctuations, adequately planning purchases, and adjusting stock levels based on consumption trends.

Automation and Robotics

Automation and robotics play an increasingly significant role in modern warehouses. Robots can handle goods, prepare orders, and contribute to reducing delivery times, improving overall efficiency.

Safety Stock Management

Maintaining an adequate level of safety stock is crucial to cope with unforeseen demand variations or delivery delays. This balance helps prevent stockouts and maintain high levels of customer service.

Omni-Channel Retailing

The integration of online and offline channels requires highly synchronized and flexible stock management. Real-time stock visibility is crucial to meet customer expectations in an omnichannel environment.

Distribution Networks and Sorting Centers

The design and optimization of distribution networks and sorting centers influence the speed and efficiency of the supply chain. The strategic location of these centers is vital to minimize transportation times and costs.

Sustainability and Waste Reduction

Sustainable practices in warehouse management include reducing packaging, recycling, using renewable energy, and minimizing waste. These approaches contribute to reducing the environmental impact of warehouse operations.

Personnel Training and Workplace Safety
Continuous staff training is essential to maintain high levels of efficiency and ensure workplace safety. The adoption of best practices and the adaptation to new technologies help create a safe and efficient working environment.
Observing the interaction of these elements, it becomes clear that inventory and warehouse management in retail is a complex process that requires a careful balance between operational efficiency, customer satisfaction, and sustainability.

Special attention in inventory and warehouse management is directed toward the implementation of artificial intelligence (AI) and machine learning systems. These technologies are becoming increasingly relevant in analyzing historical and consumer behavioral data, enabling more accurate predictions of future buying trends and optimizing inventory levels as a result. Machine learning, in particular, can analyze vast amounts of data in real-time, adapting to market variations and providing valuable insights for inventory planning.

Returns Management
Another crucial aspect is returns management, which represents an increasingly significant challenge, especially with the growth of e-

commerce. Efficient returns management, including product evaluation, repositioning in the warehouse, or potential disposal, directly impacts operational costs and customer satisfaction. Retail is, therefore, implementing innovative solutions for more effective and sustainable returns management.

Blockchain Technology

In the context of digitalization, blockchain technology is emerging as a promising tool for tracking the origin and movement of goods. This system enables the creation of an immutable and transparent transaction ledger, increasing consumer trust and reducing the risks of counterfeiting and fraud.

Shared Economy and Collaborative Platforms

In an effort to further enhance efficiency, companies are exploring new business models, such as the shared economy and collaborative platforms. These models allow for the sharing of resources, knowledge, and skills, contributing to cost reduction and increased flexibility and responsiveness to market changes.

Drones and Autonomous Vehicles

The introduction of drones and autonomous vehicles in the warehouse represents significant innovation. These devices can perform repetitive tasks in goods handling, reducing human workload and improving operational precision and speed. Experimentation in this field is progressing rapidly, and it is expected that these technologies will have an increasingly significant impact on warehouse management in the future.

Ethical and Social Responsibility

In parallel, the growing awareness of ethical and social issues is leading to the establishment of higher standards for working conditions and workers' rights. Retail is called upon to provide safe, fair, and inclusive working environments, respecting diversity and promoting employee professional development.

Virtual Reality (VR) and Augmented Reality (AR)

The implementation of virtual reality (VR) and augmented reality (AR) solutions is contributing to improved staff training and operational efficiency. These technologies offer innovative possibilities for scenario simulation, space planning, and resource management, allowing for a clearer view and a better understanding of warehouse dynamics.

Supply Chain Transparency and Real-Time Monitoring

The need for greater transparency and traceability in supply chains is driving companies to invest in advanced labeling systems and real-time monitoring platforms. These tools help ensure compliance with regulations, improve corporate social responsibility, and build stronger and more sustainable relationships with suppliers and customers.

One of the increasingly relevant challenges in inventory and warehouse management is adapting to climate change and environmental resilience. Retail businesses are taking measures to ensure that their operations are sustainable and capable of withstanding extreme weather events. This includes adapting warehouse infrastructures, using sustainable materials, and reducing carbon footprints through the use of renewable energy and eco-friendly transportation.

Another evolving area is the integration of predictive intelligence systems. Through the use of big data and advanced analytics, these solutions can predict inventory issues before they occur, enabling timely interventions and reducing the likelihood of stockouts or overstock. Moreover, personalizing customer experiences is becoming a crucial aspect of stock management. Companies use technologies such as customer behavior analysis and machine learning to predict customer preferences and customize product offerings, directly influencing purchasing and inventory decisions.

Risk management in the supply chain is another key area. Identifying and mitigating risks, such as supply chain disruptions, fluctuations in raw material prices, and demand volatility, is essential for ensuring operational continuity and protecting profit margins.

The adoption of circular economies is also an emerging trend. This model is based on using and reusing resources for as long as possible, reducing waste, and promoting recycling and material recovery. This implies inventory and warehouse management oriented toward sustainability and resource efficiency.

Animal Welfare and Ethical Practices

The growing importance of animal welfare and ethical practices in food supply chains has led companies to review their purchasing and warehousing policies. Traceability and certification of animal-origin products have become a priority to meet consumer expectations and ensure compliance with regulations.

Interconnection through the Internet of Things (IoT)

Finally, the interconnection of various management systems through the Internet of Things (IoT) is enhancing operational efficiency. Sensors and connected devices collect real-time data, providing valuable information for monitoring warehouse conditions, inventory management, and preventive equipment maintenance.

In conclusion, the complexity and speed of changes in the retail landscape demand constant innovation and adaptation in inventory and warehouse management. Companies must remain proactive and flexible, adopting new technologies and practices to address emerging challenges and meet growing consumer expectations.

Integration of Advanced Robotics

The integration of advanced robotics into the warehouse environment is becoming increasingly common. Autonomous Mobile Robots (AMRs) and Automated Storage and Retrieval Systems (AS/RS) are transforming inventory management, reducing goods handling times, and minimizing human errors. Robotics, combined with artificial vision systems, allows more efficient and accurate product picking and packaging.

Augmented Reality (AR) Technologies

Augmented reality (AR) technologies are becoming indispensable tools in warehouse management. Through devices such as smart glasses, workers can receive real-time information, navigation instructions, and visual assistance for tasks like picking, inspection, and maintenance, significantly increasing their productivity and reducing errors.

Connected Warehouse through IoT

The digital transformation has also introduced the concept of the connected warehouse. Through the Internet of Things (IoT), every element of the warehouse, from goods to shelves and handling vehicles, can be monitored in real-time. This connectivity allows for more precise stock control, better resource planning, and a faster response to demand fluctuations.

Sustainability

Sustainability is another predominant theme in inventory and warehouse management. Companies are exploring innovative solutions to reduce the environmental impact of their operations, such as the use of eco-friendly packaging materials, waste reduction through upcycling practices, and the implementation of advanced energy management systems to minimize energy consumption.

Supplier Engagement

Supplier involvement is essential for effective inventory management. Through collaborative practices and the adoption of shared digital platforms, companies can synchronize their production and distribution plans, improving visibility along the supply chain and reducing the risks of stockouts or overstock.

Safety

Another critical aspect is safety. Companies are adopting advanced technologies to ensure worker safety and prevent accidents in the warehouse. For example, motion detection and immediate alert systems can help prevent collisions between people and handling vehicles.

Flexibility in Response to Market Uncertainty

To address market uncertainty and demand fluctuations, flexibility has become an essential feature of inventory management. Cloud-based solutions and machine learning algorithms enable companies to quickly adapt their warehouse and distribution strategies in response to market changes.

Customer-Centric Approach

Finally, a customer-centric focus is at the heart of inventory management in retail. The ability to quickly and accurately meet customer needs is essential for building long-term relationships and ensuring customer loyalty. This involves a careful analysis of purchasing habits, service level optimization, and personalized offerings.

Blockchain Implementation

The implementation of blockchain is revolutionizing transparency and traceability in inventory and warehouse management. This technology allows for a secure and immutable record of transactions throughout the entire supply chain, facilitating product authenticity verification and reducing the risk of fraud and counterfeiting.

Staff Training and Development

Training and continuous education of warehouse staff have become crucial. Training courses and workshops are regularly organized to keep staff up to date with new technologies and industry best practices. Investment in human capital contributes not only to improving operational efficiency but also to increasing employee satisfaction and motivation.

Changing Warehouse Perspective

The concept of the warehouse as a cost center is changing, with many companies beginning to see the warehouse as a value-added center. This shift in perspective is leading to new strategies for optimizing warehouse space usage, improving logistical processes, and offering additional services, such as personalized packaging and product labeling.

Companies are also exploring the use of drones for warehouse management. Drones can be employed to conduct inventories, monitor product conditions, and quickly locate merchandise within the warehouse. This can significantly reduce inventory management times and improve stock data accuracy.

The implementation of Key Performance Indicator (KPI) based performance management systems is helping companies monitor and enhance warehouse efficiency. Through KPI analysis, such as order accuracy and cycle times, companies can identify areas for improvement and implement corrective actions.

Warehouse space design and optimization are becoming increasingly sophisticated, with the introduction of solutions like 3D modeling and computerized simulation. These tools allow testing different warehouse configurations and optimizing resource allocation based on each company's specific needs.

Furthermore, the growing concern for data security has led to strengthening cybersecurity measures. Companies are adopting advanced security protocols and backup solutions to protect sensitive data and ensure operational continuity in the event of cyberattacks.

Attention to the well-being and health of workers is another aspect gaining relevance in stock and warehouse management. The adoption of ergonomic technologies, promotion of healthy lifestyles, and implementation of workplace safety protocols are all initiatives contributing to creating a safe and productive work environment.

Lastly, sales forecasting's role in stock management is becoming increasingly central. The use of predictive models and historical data analysis enables anticipating market trends and planning the purchase and allocation of goods with greater precision, reducing the risk of obsolescence and ensuring product availability when and where it is needed.

In conclusion, stock and warehouse management is a key element in modern retail and is undergoing a period of rapid evolution and innovation. The introduction and implementation of new technologies such as robotics, artificial intelligence, blockchain, and drones are revolutionizing logistics processes, helping reduce costs, improve efficiency, and enhance stock management accuracy.

Focus on staff training and well-being, combined with a greater emphasis on physical and cybersecurity, is contributing to creating a safer and more productive work environment with motivated and competent employees.

The transformation of the perception of warehouses from cost centers to value-added centers underscores the strategic importance of stock management in companies' value chains. This paradigm shift is leading to new business models and opportunities to offer additional services and create value for the customer.

The adoption of advanced analytics tools and predictive models is improving companies' ability to anticipate market trends and proactively adapt to demand fluctuations, in turn reducing the risk of obsolescence and ensuring better product availability.

Moreover, the adoption of sustainable practices and engagement with suppliers through shared digital platforms highlight a growing commitment to environmental and social responsibility and the creation of more resilient and sustainable supply chains.

Finally, optimized warehouse design and innovation in space management are contributing to maximizing operational efficiency and adapting logistical infrastructure to the increasingly complex and dynamic market needs.

In summary, stock and warehouse management in modern retail is a field in constant evolution, characterized by challenges and opportunities, where technological innovation, attention to personnel and customers, sustainability, and corporate strategy intertwine to form a complex and dynamic ecosystem.

7. Merchandising and Store Layout

Merchandising and store layout are fundamental factors that influence consumer buying behavior in the modern retail sector. When strategically managed, these aspects can optimize product presentation, pique customer interest, and increase sales.

Merchandising deals with the arrangement, presentation, and promotion of products within the store. It encompasses various techniques and strategies, such as the use of promotional displays, creating hot and cold zones in the store, and the optimal placement of products on shelves to capture customer attention and encourage purchases.

On the other hand, **store layout** refers to the design and organization of the interior space, including the arrangement of shelves, promotional islands, cash registers, and service areas. A well-designed layout facilitates customer circulation, creates a pleasant atmosphere, and enhances the value of products for sale.

Visual Merchandising is a key discipline in this context. It relies on the creative use of lighting, colors, graphics, and materials to create an engaging environment and stimulate a positive shopping experience. Visual Merchandising aims to communicate the brand's identity, enhance products, and establish an emotional connection with customers.

Data analysis and artificial intelligence are becoming increasingly important tools in the field of merchandising and store layout. The use of predictive analytics, heat maps, and customer tracking data allows retailers to optimize product placement, predict buying trends, and personalize promotional offers based on consumer behavior and preferences.

Sustainability is another central theme. Retailers are adopting eco-friendly materials, reducing plastic usage, and promoting sustainable practices. Growing consumer interest in environmental and ethical concerns is influencing merchandising choices and store design, focusing on transparency, responsibility, and corporate values.

Another key element is **omnichannel**, the ability to integrate the online and offline shopping experience. Merchandising elements and store layout must be consistent with the brand's digital presence, and promotional strategies need to be integrated across various sales channels.

Moreover, **personalizing the shopping experience** is becoming increasingly relevant. Retailers are exploring technological solutions, such as smartphone apps and augmented reality, to offer personalized services, product recommendations, and targeted promotions based on customer data and buying habits.

Finally, **employee training and creating a positive work environment** are essential elements for the success of merchandising and layout strategies. A motivated and competent team can deliver quality customer service and contribute to creating a welcoming and stimulating in-store atmosphere.

One of the central aspects of merchandising is **consumer psychology**. Understanding how customers think, feel, and react is fundamental for creating a layout and product display that influences buying behavior. For example, studies have shown that products placed at eye level are more noticed and, therefore, more purchased. Similarly, the use of bright colors and focused lighting can draw attention to specific products.

Store soundscaping is another factor influencing the shopping experience. Music, volume, and sounds within the store can impact the time customers spend in the store, their mood, and, consequently, their buying behavior. Well-designed soundscaping strategies can improve the in-store atmosphere and stimulate specific emotional reactions in customers.

Even **scents** play a role in sensory merchandising. Some stores use aroma diffusers to create a pleasant and inviting olfactory environment or evoke memories and emotions that can influence purchases. For example, the scent of freshly baked bread in a supermarket can stimulate appetite and increase the sale of food products.

Furthermore, **the integration of technology** in retail stores is becoming increasingly sophisticated. In addition to augmented reality solutions and personalized apps, some retailers are experimenting with interactive screens, digital kiosks, and electronic shelf labels to provide detailed product information, customer reviews, and customization options. These technologies can also collect data on customer behavior in-store, providing valuable insights for further merchandising and layout optimization.

Assortment Management and Product Rotation

Assortment management and product rotation are crucial practices in merchandising. Maintaining a fresh and varied product assortment that caters to customer needs and desires is essential to keep interest alive and encourage customer loyalty. At the same time, it's important to balance variety with space availability and ensure that products nearing expiration or in excess stock are efficiently managed through discounts, promotions, or other sales channels.

Accessibility and Usability of Products

Accessibility and usability of products are equally fundamental. A well-designed layout facilitates navigation, reduces product search time, and improves the efficiency of the purchasing process. The use of clear signage, logical organization of product categories, and the presence of intuitive pathways contribute to creating a smooth and satisfying shopping experience.

Moreover, the layout and merchandising must consider the diverse needs of customers based on demographic, cultural, and socio-economic factors. For instance, in areas with a younger or more multicultural population, offering a diversified and innovative product assortment or using different communication and promotion strategies might be appropriate.

Flexibility and Adaptability

Finally, flexibility and adaptability are essential features of modern merchandising. The retail market is constantly evolving, with new trends, products, and customer expectations regularly emerging. Being able to quickly adapt store layout and merchandising strategies to these changes is crucial to maintain competitiveness and meet consumer needs.

In addition to the elements mentioned, **visual merchandising** is a fundamental component of store layout. It focuses on the aesthetic aspect of the point of sale, using displays, mannequins, images, and other visual elements to create an engaging environment consistent with the brand's image. Well-executed visual merchandising can increase product visibility, stimulate customer interest, and positively influence purchasing decisions.

In the context of large-scale retail, the localization and arrangement of products within the store are strategic. Essential items like milk and bread are often placed at the back of the store, encouraging customers to traverse the entire space and thereby increasing the likelihood of impulse purchases. Similarly, high-margin products are frequently positioned at eye level, while low-margin items are placed higher or lower on the shelves.

Hot and Cold Zones in the store represent another important concept. Hot zones are high-traffic areas where customers tend to linger longer, while cold zones are less frequented areas. Identifying and optimizing these zones can help maximize product exposure and increase sales.

Data analysis plays a crucial role in merchandising and store layout management. Data related to sales, customer flow, time spent in the store, and other behavioral factors can provide valuable insights to optimize product placement, assortment, and promotional strategies. The use of advanced technologies, such as geolocation and motion sensors, can further refine analysis and support informed decisions.

Sustainability in Merchandising and Store Layout

Sustainability has become an increasingly important consideration in merchandising and store layout. Modern consumers are more conscious of the environmental impact of the products they buy and the stores they frequent. Implementing sustainable practices, such as using recycled or recyclable materials for displays, optimizing lighting and energy use, and promoting eco-friendly products, can enhance the brand's image and attract environmentally conscious customers.

Moreover, the social and community aspect of stores is gaining relevance. Creating spaces for interaction and socialization, offering additional services like cafes or children's play areas, and organizing events and activities can transform the point of sale into a place for meeting and experiences, strengthening customer relationships and loyalty.

Personalization is a Growing Trend

Personalization is a growing trend in retail. Offering personalized solutions, such as tailor-made products, customizable labels, or individualized consulting services, can add value for customers and differentiate the store from the competition. Integrating technologies like 3D printing or interactive screens can support these strategies and enrich the store's offerings.

In conclusion, merchandising and store layout in large-scale retail are key elements that directly influence consumer buying behavior and, consequently, the commercial success of the point of sale. The strategic arrangement of products, effective use of hot and cold zones, data analysis, and the adoption of innovative technologies are all tactics that contribute to creating an optimized and engaging shopping environment.

The Role of Visual Merchandising

Visual merchandising, which focuses on the store's aesthetic aspect, uses various visual elements to create a consistent and stimulating shopping experience, positively influencing the brand's perception and customer decisions.

Meeting Modern Consumer Expectations

The incorporation of sustainable practices and the creation of a social and community atmosphere are also essential to meet the growing expectations of modern consumers, who seek not only products but also values and experiences.

The introduction of personalized solutions and the implementation of additional services and advanced technologies, such as 3D printing and interactive screens, offer further opportunities to differentiate from the competition and build a strong customer bond. In an increasingly competitive and evolving market, the ability to innovate and adapt merchandising and store layout to consumer needs and desires is crucial for maintaining and expanding market share.

Sustainability is Imperative

Sustainability, in particular, has become not only an added value but also an imperative, given the increasing environmental awareness among consumers. Green initiatives, the use of ecological materials, and the promotion of sustainable products not only improve the brand's image but also satisfy an increasingly discerning and informed demand.

Finally, ongoing analysis and experimentation based on reliable and up-to-date data will enable retailers to anticipate trends, adjust strategies, and offer a shopping experience that consistently meets consumer expectations, ensuring long-term success in the dynamic retail sector.

8. Private Label vs. Name Brands

The comparison between Private Label and Name Brands is a central theme in the retail industry. Private Label, or store brands, are products manufactured or supplied by third parties but sold under the retailer's brand. On the other hand, Name Brands are products made and sold under the manufacturer's brand.

Private Label

1. **Price:** Generally, Private Label products have a lower price compared to Name Brands, making them attractive to price-conscious consumers.

2. **Profit Margin:** Retailers tend to achieve higher profit margins from Private Label products.
3. **Control:** Retailers have more control over the production, quality, and marketing strategy of Private Label products.
4. **Exclusivity:** Being exclusive to a particular retailer, Private Label products can help differentiate the offering and create customer loyalty.
5. **Adaptability:** Private Label products can be quickly adapted to meet market needs and consumer trends.

Name Brands

1. **Brand Recognition:** Name Brands enjoy high recognition and a well-established reputation, which can result in greater consumer trust.
2. **Marketing and Advertising:** Name Brands invest significantly in marketing and advertising, increasing demand and often justifying higher prices.
3. **Innovation:** Name Brands are often at the forefront of research and development, regularly launching new products and innovations.
4. **Wide Distribution:** Name Brand products are generally available in a variety of retail outlets, increasing their visibility and accessibility.

In summary, both Private Label and Name Brands have unique advantages and challenges. Retailers must carefully consider their strategy for these two types of products, balancing factors such as price, quality, brand control, and customer loyalty, to optimize their offering and meet the diverse needs of consumers.

Market Development: Over the years, the Private Label market has grown exponentially. Initially associated with low-quality and low-cost products, these items have undergone a transformation, with retailers now offering premium and specialized options, attracting a broader and more diverse customer base. Similarly, Name Brands continue to explore new market segments and diversify their offerings to maintain relevance and competitiveness.

Consumer Trust: Consumer perception and trust play a crucial role in the success of both Private Label and Name Brands. Online reviews, product rankings, and quality certifications have increased visibility and transparency, influencing purchasing decisions and building or destroying brand reputation.

Sustainability and Social Responsibility: In an era where sustainability is in the spotlight, both Private Label and Name Brands are investing in environmentally sustainable practices, ethical production, and eco-friendly packaging. These efforts not only respond to growing consumer expectations but also contribute to building a positive and responsible brand image.

Customization and Differentiation:

Customizing products and adapting to local preferences have become key factors in creating value. Private Label, having direct control over production and marketing, can easily experiment with new formulations and varieties, while Name Brands can leverage their expertise and market knowledge to introduce targeted innovations.

Pricing and Promotion Strategies:

Price dynamics between Private Label and Name Brands are continually evolving. While promotions and discounts are common tools to stimulate sales, the adoption of dynamic and personalized pricing strategies, based on advanced data analysis, is becoming increasingly prevalent.

Technological Adoption:

The use of technology, such as artificial intelligence, big data analysis, and augmented reality, is shaping consumer-product interactions. These technologies allow for greater personalization of the shopping experience and a better understanding of consumer habits and preferences.

Collaborations and Partnerships:

Market evolution has also seen an increase in collaborations between Private Label and Name Brands. These partnerships can involve the sharing of production resources, marketing expertise, or distribution channels, creating synergies and mutually beneficial opportunities. In this rapidly evolving context, both Private Label and Name Brands are challenged to remain agile, constantly innovate, and adapt to changing consumer needs and expectations. The depth and complexity of this environment require careful observation and a well-considered strategy to successfully navigate the landscape of retail.

Further Exploration in the World of Private Label and Name Brands:

Effects of Globalization: Globalization has had a significant impact on product distribution. Name Brands, with their global presence, have gained access to new markets and consumers. At the same time, Private Label has benefited from the opportunity to produce in countries with lower production costs while maintaining high quality standards.

Price Wars: The market is often the scene of price wars, especially when economies of scale and mass production come into play. Name Brands, to maintain their market share, may decide to lower prices, prompting Private Label to reconsider their pricing strategies to remain competitive.

Customer Loyalty: Customer loyalty strategies have become increasingly sophisticated and central. Loyalty programs, loyalty cards, and exclusive offers are tools used by both Private Label and Name Brands to maintain and increase their customer base.

Brand Reputation and Image: Brand image and reputation are invaluable assets for both. While Name Brands often invest substantial sums in advertising, Private Label relies on quality and customer satisfaction to build and maintain their reputation.

Consumer Trends: Monitoring consumer trends is fundamental for both parties. Understanding consumer habits, preferences, and values helps both Private Label and Name Brands adapt their products and marketing strategies.

Regulations and Certifications: Compliance with rigorous regulations and obtaining quality certifications are essential to gain consumer trust. Both Name Brands and Private Label invest in this area, ensuring compliance with the highest standards.

Data Analysis and Market Intelligence: The importance of data analysis cannot be underestimated. The ability to collect, analyze, and act on consumer data is fundamental for personalizing offers, predicting trends, and optimizing sales strategies.

Resilience and Agility: In an ever-changing market, resilience and agility are key to success. The ability to adapt quickly to market changes, economic shocks, and global crises determines the long-term sustainability of both Private Label and Name Brands.

These additional layers of complexity add depth to the Private Label vs. Name Brands conversation, highlighting the need for a holistic view and a carefully articulated strategy to successfully navigate this ever-evolving industry.

Further Exploration in the Competition between Private Label and Name Brands:
Exploring how product innovation, sustainability, and corporate social responsibility influence consumer perception and, consequently, a brand's success in the market is essential.

Product Innovation:
The ability to introduce innovative products is crucial. Name Brands often have significant budgets for Research and Development, allowing them to launch groundbreaking products. On the other hand, Private Label brands tend to be quick in adopting innovations, offering cost-effective alternatives.

Environmental Sustainability:
The growing environmental awareness among consumers has led to increased interest in sustainable products. Both Name Brands and Private Label brands are seeking to reduce their environmental impact by using recyclable materials, reducing carbon emissions, and adopting ethical production practices.
Corporate Social Responsibility (CSR):
CSR has become an essential component of business management. Companies engage in social, educational, and environmental initiatives, not only to enhance their brand image but also to build strong relationships with the community and consumers.
Communication Channels:
With the advent of social media and digital marketing, communication channels have multiplied. Online presence, influencer marketing campaigns, and online review management are all strategies employed by both Private Label and Name Brands to reach and engage their audience.
Positioning Strategies:
The positioning of a product or brand in the market is crucial. While Name Brands can focus on quality, exclusivity, and innovation, Private Label brands can compete with affordable prices, offering a good value proposition.

Product Differentiation:
Differentiation is essential to avoid
commoditization. Introducing unique features,
distinctive designs, and innovative packaging are
all methods used to stand out from the
competition and capture consumer attention.
Collaborations and Partnerships:
Both Private Label and Name Brands seek
strategic collaborations and partnerships. These
can include collaborations with renowned
designers, partnerships with technology
companies, or initiatives with non-profit
organizations for social responsibility projects.
Consumer Feedback:
Listening to consumer feedback is essential for
adapting products and strategies. Creating open
communication channels and analyzing reviews
and surveys allow companies to meet the needs
and expectations of the market.
Exploring these additional aspects provides an
even more detailed view of the dynamics and
challenges that characterize the relationship
between Private Label and Name Brands,
emphasizing the complexity and variety of factors
that influence their success in the modern
market.
In conclusion, the comparison between Private
Label and Name Brands represents a
fundamental dynamic in the modern retail

landscape, where the balance between quality, price, and perceived value is constantly at play. The distinction between these two types of brands has become less pronounced, thanks to Private Label's ability to elevate their quality standards and diversify their offerings, and simultaneously, to Name Brands adopting more aggressive and flexible pricing strategies. Branding, marketing, and positioning strategies have become central for both in order to create a lasting connection with the consumer and build a strong reputation in the market.

Product innovation continues to be a relevant point of contention, with Name Brands often pioneering the launch of new products and technologies, while Private Label brands are quick to adapt and offer cost-effective alternatives. Sustainability and social responsibility have become not just an added value but an essential requirement, significantly influencing consumer choices and, therefore, the competition between brands.

Furthermore, the evolution of communication channels and the growing importance of the digital realm have led to a renewed focus on consumer engagement strategies. Customer interaction, continuous feedback, and a presence on social media are key factors for loyalty and the construction of a strong and recognizable brand.

Differentiation, through the creation of unique products, captivating designs, and innovative packaging, remains a cornerstone of brand strategy, essential for standing out in an increasingly saturated and diverse market. At the same time, collaborations and partnerships prove to be strategic tools, creating synergies and opportunities for mutual growth.

In the end, the rivalry between Private Label and Name Brands is a symptom of a constantly changing market, where adaptability, innovation, and building relationships with consumers are essential for long-term success. Understanding the dynamics, consumer expectations, and market trends is therefore crucial for successfully navigating the complex and competitive world of modern retail.

9. Pricing Strategies

Exploring the theme of pricing strategies in retail, we delve into a central aspect that determines a company's competitiveness in the market. Pricing strategies directly impact profit margins, consumer perceived value, and a

company or product's market position. Various
methodologies and approaches are adopted
based on business objectives, market
characteristics, and consumer behavior.

1. **Penetration Pricing:** This strategy involves
   initially setting low prices to attract customers
   and rapidly gain market share. Once achieved,
   prices can be increased.
2. **Skimming Pricing:** In contrast, skimming
   strategy involves setting high prices for new
   products to maximize profits from initial sales
   and then gradually reducing prices over time.
3. **Psychological Pricing:** This strategy exploits
   consumer psychology by setting prices at levels
   that consumers perceive as lower, such as €9.99
   instead of €10.00.
4. **Dynamic Pricing:** Dynamic pricing involves
   adjusting prices in real-time based on variables
   like demand, supply, consumer behavior, or
   market conditions.
5. **Promotional Pricing:** This strategy entails
   offering discounts, deals, and promotions to
   stimulate sales, attract new customers, or clear
   inventory.
6. **Cost-Based Pricing:** In this case, the price is
   determined by adding a profit margin to the total
   production and distribution costs.

7. **Value-Based Pricing:** This strategy sets prices based on the perceived value by the consumer, rather than production costs.
8. **Competitive Pricing:** Here, prices are set in relation to competitors' prices, which can be matched, undercut, or surpassed depending on objectives.
9. **Geographic Pricing:** This strategy considers price differences in various geographic areas due to variations in transport costs, taxes, or market conditions.
10. **Bundle Pricing:** Bundling involves offering multiple products or services together at a reduced price compared to separate purchases. These diverse strategies are often combined and adapted based on specific market needs and competitive dynamics. It is essential for businesses to understand the context in which they operate, continuously analyze consumer behavior, and monitor competitors' moves to adopt the most effective pricing strategy. The goal is to maximize profits, increase market share, strengthen the brand's position, and build lasting customer relationships.

The world of pricing strategies is incredibly intricate and continually evolving in response to market changes, consumer trends, and technological innovation. For example, the rise of e-commerce has introduced new dynamics and challenges in pricing, making the market even more competitive and transparent. Consumers, equipped with increasingly advanced digital tools, can compare prices in real-time, read reviews, and obtain discounts, thus altering their expectations and buying behavior.

Another fundamental aspect to consider is the impact of online reviews and social media on value perception. The reputation of a product or brand can significantly influence a consumer's willingness to pay a certain price. Therefore, companies are called upon to carefully manage their online image and engage with consumers by listening to feedback and resolving any issues. Price personalization represents an emerging trend, where consumer data analysis allows companies to offer differentiated prices based on each customer's preferences, buying behavior, and price sensitivity. This approach can help optimize profit margins but also raises ethical and privacy issues that need to be carefully managed.

Furthermore, the increasing focus on sustainability is influencing pricing strategies. Consumers are becoming more aware of the environmental and social impact of the products they purchase and are willing to pay a premium for ethically and sustainably produced goods. As a result, companies are exploring pricing models that reflect these values and are proactively communicating their sustainability efforts.

An additional aspect to explore is the importance of price transparency. Consumers today want to understand the composition of the final price and what factors contribute to the product's cost. Greater transparency can enhance customer trust and strengthen the brand's connection with its customers.
Finally, it is essential to emphasize that pricing strategy is not static but dynamic and adaptable. Companies must constantly monitor sales performance, analyze consumer reactions, and be prepared to adjust the pricing strategy in response to new market opportunities or challenges. The ability to adapt and innovate is crucial in an increasingly complex and evolving business environment.
In the context of retail, pricing strategies intersect with competition dynamics and market peculiarities. It is essential to explore how pricing strategies can be used to increase market share, attract new customers, and retain existing customers.
A common practice is that of psychological pricing, which involves setting prices that end in .99 or .95. This technique is based on consumer perception and the idea that a price of €9.99 is

significantly lower than €10.00, even though the actual difference is minimal. This strategy can positively influence the perception of value and increase sales.

Promoting sales through discounts, special offers, and loyalty programs is another key mechanism in the retail context. These tools stimulate demand and increase sales volume, although they may erode profit margins. Effective management of promotions requires a careful analysis of consumer behavior and demand elasticity.

The concept of perceived value also plays a crucial role in pricing strategies. Companies seek to position their products in a way that consumers perceive an optimal value for money. The goal is to create a balance between the perceived value by the consumer and the actual price of the product, thus influencing the propensity to purchase.

Dynamic pricing, the ability to adjust prices in real-time based on variables such as demand, supply, and market conditions, is another growing strategy, particularly relevant in e-commerce. This practice allows for profit maximization and flexible responses to market fluctuations.

Competitive price analysis is also fundamental. Companies constantly monitor competitors' prices and adapt their pricing strategy based on their desired market positioning. This may include adopting penetration strategies with initially low prices to gain market share or premium pricing to position the product as high-quality.

Furthermore, it is crucial to consider the impact of pricing strategies on the brand and the corporate image. Consistent price positioning with the brand's identity helps reinforce the perception of value and build a lasting connection with consumers.

Finally, in an era of increasing digitalization and globalization, it is essential to explore how pricing strategies can be adapted to different markets and customer segments, taking into account cultural differences, local regulations, and consumer expectations.

In the context of pricing strategies in retail, it is also essential to examine the impact of digital technologies and big data. Access to vast amounts of consumer data allows companies to refine their pricing strategies, segment their offerings, and personalize prices in ways previously impossible. For example, technology enables the analysis of consumer purchasing behavior and preferences, allowing for targeted promotions and discounts, as well as price optimization for different customer segments.

Another relevant aspect is price transparency. With the advent of the internet and price comparison platforms, consumers can increasingly compare product prices among different retailers. This transparency compels companies to be more competitive and find a balance between attractive prices and sustainable profit margins.

Dynamic pricing and yield management strategies are particularly relevant in this context. These strategies allow prices to be adjusted in real-time in response to changes in demand and supply, thus optimizing revenues. For example, prices can be increased during periods of high demand or reduced to clear inventory.

Furthermore, it is important to consider the importance of price consistency across various distribution channels. Companies operate in an omnichannel environment where consumers purchase products both online and offline. Maintaining price consistency across different channels is crucial to avoid confusion and customer dissatisfaction and to maintain a strong and coherent brand image.

Sustainability is another central theme in contemporary pricing strategies. Consumers are increasingly aware of environmental and social issues and are willing to pay a premium for sustainable products. Therefore, companies can adopt pricing strategies that reflect these preferences, positioning sustainable products at a premium price and effectively communicating their environmental and social benefits.

Psychological considerations also influence consumer behavior and, consequently, pricing strategies. Neuromarketing techniques, for example, study consumer reactions to various stimuli, including prices, to understand the factors influencing purchasing decisions and to develop more effective pricing strategies.

Not to be overlooked is the impact of regulations and tax policies on pricing strategies. Companies must navigate a complex and ever-changing regulatory environment where factors such as taxes, customs duties, and competition regulations can significantly influence product prices and profit margins.

In conclusion, defining pricing strategies in retail is a complex and multifaceted process that requires a careful balance between internal and external factors and continuous adaptability to market dynamics.

In the context of pricing strategies in retail, it is also essential to consider the peculiarities of different geographical markets. Factors such as purchasing power, local competition, and consumer preferences vary significantly from one region to another, necessitating a differentiated and localized approach. Retail companies, especially those with international presence, must develop flexible and adaptable pricing strategies tailored to diverse market realities.

The role of competitors is also crucial in shaping pricing strategies. The presence of rivals practicing aggressive pricing can force companies to reduce margins to maintain competitiveness, while a context with less competition can offer greater opportunities for differentiation through pricing. Competitive analysis and monitoring of competitor prices are therefore central activities in defining pricing strategies.

The growth of e-commerce has introduced additional challenges and opportunities in terms of pricing strategies. Online commerce allows for greater price customization through the collection and analysis of user data. However, it also entails increased price comparison by consumers and the need to integrate online and offline pricing strategies.

The psychological leverage of price is also of great importance. Pricing strategies can leverage various psychological mechanisms, such as charm pricing (prices ending in .99), to influence the perception of value and stimulate purchases. Understanding consumer psychology and applying psychological pricing techniques can significantly contribute to the success of pricing strategies.

Innovation in payment methods is another factor that influences pricing strategies. The adoption of new payment systems, such as cryptocurrencies or contactless payments, can have implications on price dynamics and consumer expectations. Companies must keep an eye on payment trends and adjust their pricing strategies accordingly.

Cost management is fundamental in shaping pricing strategies. Companies must continually monitor and optimize production, distribution, and marketing costs to maintain healthy margins and offer competitive prices. Operational efficiency and cost reduction can enable companies to offer lower prices without eroding profitability.

Lastly, the importance of ethics and social responsibility in pricing strategies cannot be underestimated. Companies are increasingly called upon to respond to sustainability and equity needs, and pricing strategies must reflect these values. Ethical and responsible pricing can help build a positive reputation and create long-term value for the company.

In conclusion, the art of pricing strategies in retail is a multidimensional practice that requires a holistic and well-considered approach. The ability to balance costs, meet consumer expectations, monitor and respond to competition, and effectively integrate online and offline channels are key elements in formulating winning pricing strategies.

Pricing strategies are not static but dynamic and ever-evolving. Companies must quickly adapt to market changes, fluctuations in raw material costs, new technologies, and evolving consumer behaviors. The use of advanced data analysis and market intelligence tools is therefore crucial for predicting trends and optimizing pricing strategies in real-time.

Furthermore, it is essential that retail companies align their pricing strategies with long-term business goals and make them an integral part of an overall marketing and positioning strategy. Price is one of the key elements of the marketing mix and directly influences consumer perceptions of value. A well-formulated and consistent pricing strategy is therefore essential for the success and sustainability of a company in the competitive arena of modern retail.

All of this underscores the importance of in-depth analysis, continuous market monitoring, and ongoing skill and knowledge development to develop and implement effective pricing strategies in the dynamic world of modern retail.

10. Marketing and Advertising

Marketing and advertising in the retail sector are fundamental pillars for the success of businesses. These elements serve to create brand awareness, generate traffic in physical and online retail locations, and encourage consumer purchases.

1. **Differentiated Marketing Strategies:** Retail businesses adopt differentiated marketing strategies to reach diverse customer segments. The use of techniques such as sensory marketing, visual merchandising, and experiential marketing contributes to creating a unique experience for the consumer.
2. **Omnichannel Marketing:** Integration between physical and digital channels is essential. Companies use online platforms, apps, social media, and physical stores to offer a seamless and integrated customer experience, enhancing product visibility and accessibility.
3. **Offer Personalization:** Customer data analysis allows for the personalization of offers and promotions. Market segmentation and the use of advanced algorithms enable tailored products and discounts for different consumer types.
4. **Creative and Innovative Advertising:** Creating original and captivating advertising campaigns is essential to capture consumer attention. The use of influencers, storytelling, and interactive multimedia content are increasingly prevalent techniques.

5. **Sustainability and Social Responsibility:** Promoting sustainable and responsible practices has become a key element in marketing. Companies highlight their efforts in terms of environmental sustainability, labor ethics, and social contribution to build a positive image and attract conscious consumers.

6. **Loyalty and Retention Programs:** Retail companies develop loyalty programs offering benefits, exclusive discounts, and rewards to encourage customer loyalty and stimulate repeat purchases.

7. **Events and Sponsorships:** Organizing events and participating in sponsorships increases brand visibility and creates opportunities for direct interaction with consumers, strengthening customer relationships.

8. **Market Analysis and Research:** Conducting market research and analyzing sales data are essential to understand trends, consumer needs, and the effectiveness of marketing and advertising campaigns.

9. **SEO and SEM:** Search engine optimization (SEO) and search engine marketing (SEM) strategies are crucial to increase online visibility and attract qualified traffic to e-commerce websites.

10. **Public Relations and Reputation Management:** Managing public relations and

maintaining online and offline reputation are essential to uphold a positive corporate image and manage potential communication crises.

In conclusion, marketing and advertising in retail are indispensable tools that, if used strategically and innovatively, can significantly contribute to a company's success in today's competitive landscape. Adapting to new trends, paying attention to consumer needs, and adopting ethical and sustainable practices are key aspects of building lasting customer relationships and consolidating a company's market position.

In the retail sector, the continuous refinement of marketing and advertising strategies is essential to maintain competitiveness. Market dynamics evolve rapidly, and companies must stay updated on a range of relevant topics:

11. Digital Marketing: Digital marketing plays a crucial role in attracting customers online. Strategies such as content marketing, email marketing, and advertising retargeting help keep customers engaged and convert interests into purchases.

12. Big Data and Analytics: Implementing big data and analytics technologies allows the analysis of consumer behaviors and preferences, optimizing target segmentation and improving the effectiveness of advertising campaigns.

11. Collaborations and Partnerships:
Forming strategic alliances and partnerships
with other brands can expand the reach and
impact of marketing campaigns, offering mutual
benefits and access to new market segments. **12.
User Experience (UX) and Design:**
Excellent user experience in online and physical
retail locations is essential. Intuitive and
captivating design of websites, apps, and physical
store layouts can enhance customer satisfaction
and boost sales.

13. Product Innovation: Promoting
innovative new products and adapting the
product assortment to changes in consumer
preferences are essential tactics to maintain
interest and stimulate demand.

**14. Customer Relationship Management
(CRM):** Adopting advanced CRM systems allows
for managing and analyzing customer
interactions, improving customer relationships,
and increasing retention.

15. Social Media Marketing: Active presence
on social media is vital. Creating engaging
content, interacting with the audience, and
listening to online conversations can strengthen
the brand and enhance reputation.

16. Guerilla Marketing: Using unconventional
and cost-effective guerilla marketing techniques

can generate buzz and visibility, surprising the audience and making the brand memorable.

17. Influencer Marketing: Collaborating with influencers and well-known personalities can increase brand credibility and visibility, reaching specific demographic segments and creating engagement.

18. Responding to Consumer Behavior Change: Monitoring and adapting to changes in buying behavior and consumer expectations is crucial. Customer feedback and flexibility in strategies are essential to meet evolving needs.

By implementing and continually updating these strategies and techniques, retail companies can maintain their relevance in the market, attract new customers, and retain existing ones, while adapting to emerging trends and new competitive challenges. The key to success lies in the ability to innovate and customize the marketing and advertising approach in response to market dynamics and consumer preferences.

Marketing and advertising strategies in the retail industry are multifaceted and ever-evolving. In addition to the points already discussed, there are various other aspects that companies consider to remain competitive and reach their audience:

19. Sustainability and Social Responsibility: Growing attention to sustainability and social responsibility is influencing consumer choices. Companies are adopting eco-friendly and ethical practices and communicating these values through targeted marketing campaigns.

20. Loyalty Programs: Developing and managing effective loyalty programs is essential to incentivize customers to return. Points, discounts, and personalized rewards contribute to building a loyal relationship between the brand and the consumer.

21. Events and Sponsorships: Participating in industry events or sponsoring local initiatives can increase brand visibility and create positive connections with the community and potential customers.

22. Augmented Reality Technologies: Using augmented reality technologies in marketing offers an immersive shopping experience, allowing customers to virtually try products before making a purchase.

23. Personalization: Personalizing offers and communications through customer data analysis is essential to increase the relevance and effectiveness of advertising campaigns.

24. Omnichannel Marketing: Integrating the shopping experience across online and offline channels is vital. A seamless experience between websites, mobile apps, and physical stores can enhance customer satisfaction.

25 SEO and SEM: Optimizing online presence through Search Engine Optimization (SEO) and Search Engine Marketing (SEM) techniques is crucial to improve visibility on search engines and attract qualified traffic.

26. Review Management: Monitoring and responding to online reviews can improve the brand's reputation, resolve any issues, and demonstrate a commitment to customer satisfaction.

27. Storytelling: Creating and sharing engaging stories about the brand, products, or company's mission can create an emotional connection with consumers and reinforce the brand's image.

28. Video Marketing: Developing creative and informative video content can improve engagement, raise brand awareness, and encourage sharing on social channels.

By exploring and experimenting with these approaches, retail companies can discover new opportunities to connect with the audience, adapt to consumer needs, and stay at the forefront in an ever-evolving market. A combination of traditional and innovative strategies can lead to an effective marketing mix that addresses the challenges of the contemporary business landscape.

In conclusion, marketing and advertising in modern retail are essential tools for acquiring and retaining customers, increasing sales, and strengthening the brand's presence in the market. The continuous evolution of consumer preferences, the advent of new technologies, and growing competition make the adoption of innovative and diversified strategies crucial.

Sustainability and social responsibility, for example, are no longer optional but key elements in building a positive brand image and meeting the expectations of modern consumers. Personalizing offers through in-depth customer data analysis enables the creation of targeted advertising campaigns, thus increasing effectiveness and ROI.

Technologies such as augmented reality and online platforms offer new opportunities for customer interaction and sales, integrating and enhancing the traditional shopping experience. An omnichannel approach is essential in this context to ensure a seamless transition between the online and offline worlds.

Furthermore, strategies like video marketing and storytelling allow for the creation of an emotional connection with consumers, improving engagement and brand loyalty. Active review management and participation in events and sponsorships contribute to solidifying the company's reputation and visibility.

The effectiveness of marketing and advertising strategies in retail depends on the ability to combine traditional and innovative elements, quickly adapt to market changes, and anticipate consumer needs. In-depth knowledge of the target audience, the adoption of advanced technologies, and the promotion of ethical and sustainable principles are the pillars on which to build successful campaigns in the modern retail landscape.

11. Customer Loyalty (Loyalty Programs, Reward Cards, etc.)

The concept of customer loyalty in the retail sector represents a crucial component. Loyalty programs, reward cards, exclusive discounts, and other promotional initiatives are key tools to encourage customers to return and prefer a specific chain or store over competitors.

Loyalty programs, in particular, are designed to offer benefits to regular customers, such as accumulating points or receiving exclusive discounts and offers. These programs are often personalized based on customer demographics and purchasing behaviors, allowing for tailored rewards and benefits.

Reward cards are a common tool that allows customers to accumulate points for each purchase, which can then be converted into discounts, purchase vouchers, or rewards. This system not only promotes loyalty but also increases the average spend per customer.

The implementation of apps and digital platforms has further expanded possibilities in loyalty efforts. Through apps, customers can access personalized offers, participate in games and contests, receive notifications of exclusive discounts, and more, all aimed at strengthening the bond between the customer and the store. Furthermore, customer feedback collected through these channels can be used to further enhance offerings and services, contributing to a virtuous cycle of continuous improvement and customer loyalty.

It's also important to highlight the role of Customer Experience in the loyalty process. A positive shopping experience, including excellent customer service, easy in-store or online navigation, and the availability of quality products, can significantly influence the customer's perception and likelihood to return. The role of Corporate Social Responsibility (CSR) is another aspect to consider. Eco-sustainable, ethical, and social initiatives can contribute to creating a positive brand image, influencing consumer choices, and contributing to their loyalty.

In summary, customer loyalty in modern retail is a multifactorial process that requires the integration of both classic and innovative strategies, with the aim of creating a lasting and mutually beneficial bond between the customer and the company.

Technology plays an increasingly significant role in the customer loyalty process. Artificial intelligence and data analysis are employed to better identify and understand customer behaviors, allowing companies to personalize offers and communicate more effectively. This data-driven approach enables the anticipation of customer needs and the proposal of solutions aligned with their expectations.

Omnichannel strategies have become fundamental in modern retail. The goal is to provide a seamless and integrated shopping experience across all channels, both online and offline. Consistency across various channels is essential to maintain customer trust and loyalty, as customers expect the same level of service and quality regardless of their interaction with the brand.

Another important strategy in customer loyalty is the creation of communities and social media interaction. Social platforms offer the opportunity to build closer relationships with customers, promote engagement and sharing, and create a sense of belonging to the brand. User-generated content, such as reviews and testimonials, can contribute to strengthening the company's reputation and building trust with customers.

Personal branding and sales staff training are also crucial. Competent, courteous, and helpful staff can significantly improve the shopping experience and increase the likelihood of customer return. Continuous staff training and investment in human resources are therefore essential aspects of customer loyalty.

The importance of personalized offerings cannot be underestimated. Personalization solutions, supported by AI and data analysis, allow for tailored promotions, product recommendations, and individualized communications. This customer-centric approach contributes to improving satisfaction and retention.

Lastly, the integration of social and environmental responsibility programs into customer loyalty strategies can help meet the growing expectations of consumers regarding sustainability and corporate ethics. Commitment to green and social initiatives can be a differentiating factor and add value to the brand.

In conclusion, to achieve success in customer loyalty, it's essential to adopt a holistic and integrated approach that combines technological innovation, personalized marketing strategies, service excellence, and social responsibility.

In modern retail, the concept of customer loyalty is continually evolving, and companies are called upon to renew their strategies to maintain consumer interest and loyalty. The introduction of augmented and virtual reality technologies offers new possibilities to enhance the shopping experience, making it more engaging and interactive. For example, some applications allow customers to virtually view products in their home environment before making a purchase, providing added value and an additional reason to prefer a particular retailer.

Partnerships with other brands and companies can also be an effective way to increase customer loyalty. By collaborating with complementary brands, retailers can offer cross-promotions, expanding the variety of benefits available to loyal customers and encouraging them to continue shopping.

In the retail landscape, gamification dynamics are gaining ground as a loyalty tool. The idea is to incorporate playful elements into marketing strategies, such as contests, rewards, and challenges, to stimulate customer engagement and encourage them to interact with the brand more frequently and deeply.

Transparency and honesty in communication are fundamental for building a trusting relationship between the customer and the company. Clear information about the origin, composition, and production methods of products can make a difference in consumer perception, contributing to the creation of a positive brand image.

Companies are also recognizing the importance of speed and convenience in the purchasing process. Investments in fast and secure payment systems, efficient delivery services, and flexible return options are essential to meet the needs of modern customers and maintain their loyalty.

The collection and analysis of customer feedback represent another crucial aspect of loyalty. Listening to customer opinions and needs allows for targeted improvements and demonstrates that the company is genuinely interested in meeting customer expectations.

Additionally, the value of humanity and empathy in customer service cannot be overlooked. A human and personalized approach to customer service that goes beyond automation can generate a sense of appreciation and emotional connection, essential for long-term loyalty.

In addition to what has already been discussed, the concept of Corporate Social Responsibility (CSR) plays a significant role in customer loyalty. Modern consumers are increasingly attentive to the environmental and social impact of the companies they buy from. Green initiatives, sustainable packaging, ethical working conditions, and donations to charitable organizations can enhance the positive perception of the brand and influence purchasing decisions.

Personalizing offerings is another key element. Data analysis and machine learning technologies allow for the collection and analysis of customer purchase data and preferences, enabling the creation of tailored offers and promotions that meet the specific needs of each individual. This focus on personalization can result in greater satisfaction and, consequently, increased loyalty.

Online Communities and Social Media in Customer Loyalty

Online communities and social media are fundamental tools for creating and maintaining the relationship with customers. Through platforms like Facebook, Instagram, and Twitter, companies can directly interact with their customers, respond to comments, share interesting content, and initiate discussions. This direct and authentic interaction contributes to building a sense of belonging and strengthening the bond with the brand.

Continuous training and development of sales and customer service staff are essential for delivering quality service and conveying competence and reliability. Well-trained and courteous staff can make a difference in the shopping experience and contribute to building a positive reputation.

The ease of access to detailed and transparent information about products and services is another factor that contributes to customer loyalty. A well-organized website with an extensive FAQ section and easy access to customer support can increase consumer trust in the brand.

Finally, it's important not to underestimate the importance of consistency at every customer touchpoint. From the in-store experience to online navigation, from customer support to social media communication, maintaining a high and consistent level of service is crucial for building and maintaining customer trust and loyalty.

In conclusion, customer loyalty in modern retail is a multifaceted process that integrates various elements and strategies, from personalized offerings to the use of social media to corporate social responsibility. A key factor is the ability to establish and nurture a continuous and meaningful relationship with the customer. Through loyalty programs, reward cards, and other personalized initiatives, companies can create a direct and lasting bond with consumers that goes beyond individual commercial transactions. This bond is further strengthened when companies demonstrate ethical and social commitment, meeting the growing expectations of consumers in terms of sustainability and responsibility.

Technology and digital innovation play an increasingly significant role in this context. Data analysis and machine learning allow for a deep understanding of customer needs and preferences, offering them increasingly tailored products and services. At the same time, online platforms and social media provide new spaces for interaction and dialogue, enriching the customer experience and contributing to building an active and engaged community.

The role of staff, ongoing training, and excellence in customer service are equally crucial. Courteous, competent, and reliable service can significantly influence the brand's perception and customer satisfaction, laying the foundation for a long-term relationship.

Finally, transparency and accessibility of information, consistency at every touchpoint, and the ability to offer a consistent and high-quality experience, both online and offline, are fundamental elements for gaining and maintaining customer trust.

In conclusion, customer loyalty is an essential strategic element for modern retail, requiring a holistic approach and the integration of various skills and resources, from technology to ethics, from communication to training, in order to create value and ensure long-term success in the increasingly competitive and dynamic retail market.

12. Consumer Behavior Analysis

Consumer behavior analysis is a fundamental element in the field of modern retail, focusing on how individuals make decisions regarding the purchase of goods and services. This analysis is vital for companies that want to understand and predict the needs and preferences of their customers in order to offer more targeted and appealing products and services.

1. **Research Methodologies:** Consumer behavior analysis employs various research methodologies such as surveys, interviews, direct observation, and historical transaction analysis. Big Data Analysis and machine learning technology are increasingly used tools to collect and interpret vast amounts of data related to purchasing behavior.

2. **Psychological Factors:** Factors such as motivation, perception, learning, and attitude significantly influence consumer purchasing decisions. For example, advertising and marketing aim to influence a consumer's attitude toward a product or service, which, in turn, can affect their purchasing decision.

3. **Social and Cultural Factors:** Culture, social class, reference groups, and family also influence purchasing behavior. For example, a person's

eating habits can be strongly influenced by the culture they grew up in.

4. **Economic Factors:** Income, prices, and the overall economic situation are determining factors in purchasing behavior. For example, during an economic recession, consumers may be more inclined to seek low-cost products.

5. **Personal Factors:** Age, profession, personality, and lifestyle are all factors that can influence purchasing choices. For example, a person working in a creative industry may be more inclined to purchase fashionable and designer clothing.

6. **Decision-Making Process:** Understanding the stages of the consumer decision-making process, from recognizing the need, to information search, to evaluating alternatives, to the purchase decision, and finally to post-purchase behavior, is essential for companies that want to effectively influence this process in their favor.

7. **Technology and Online Behavior:** The advent of the Internet and digital technologies has significantly influenced consumer behavior. The analysis of online searches, clicks, reviews, and social media provides valuable insights into consumer preferences and purchase intentions.

8. **Sustainability and Ethics:** Growing awareness of environmental and social issues has

led to increased demand for sustainable and ethical products. Companies must take these values into account when developing products and marketing strategies.

9. **Customization and Personalization:** The expectation of tailored products and services is on the rise. Consumer behavior analysis can help companies customize their offerings to meet specific customer needs, thereby improving customer satisfaction and loyalty.

10. **Emotional Influence:** Emotions play a crucial role in purchasing decisions. Companies use emotional marketing techniques to create emotional connections with consumers and influence their choices.

In conclusion, consumer behavior analysis is a multidisciplinary field that integrates psychology, sociology, economics, and other disciplines to gain a deep understanding of consumer motivations, desires, and needs. This understanding allows companies to develop more effective strategies, customize products and services, and build long-term relationships with customers in a constantly evolving and increasingly competitive market.

Further Analyzing Consumer Behavior, it is evident that the impact of the digital era and social platforms on purchasing decision processes is significant. Online reviews, social media comments, and the influence of bloggers and influencers have an increasingly predominant role in consumer choices. The online reputation of a product or service can determine its success or failure, making online reputation monitoring and management essential activities for businesses.

In the context of online behavior, behavioral data analysis becomes crucial. The use of cookies and other tracking technologies enables companies to gather detailed data on consumers' browsing habits, allowing the creation of detailed profiles and personalization of offerings based on past behaviors and expressed preferences. Furthermore, advancements in technology have allowed for the development of neuromarketing techniques, which analyze the brain's responses to advertising messages and products. This approach delves into consumers' subconscious reactions, offering valuable insights on optimizing advertising messages for maximizing emotional and persuasive impact.

Another noteworthy aspect is the importance of convenience and usability in the purchasing process. Modern consumers tend to prioritize solutions that save time and effort, placing value on services such as home delivery, online purchase with in-store pickup, and mobile apps that facilitate price comparison and product information search.

Attention to sustainability and ethics extends beyond the purchase of eco-friendly products and includes the evaluation of corporate ethics. Informed and conscious consumers increasingly prefer companies that demonstrate commitment to social, environmental, and employee welfare issues. This trend has led to the emergence of ethical certifications and labels that companies can obtain to showcase their dedication in these areas.

Additionally, the expectation of unique and memorable shopping experiences is driving businesses to implement innovative solutions in retail stores, such as augmented and virtual reality, cashierless stores, and immersive environments, aiming to provide consumers with a shopping experience that goes beyond a simple commercial transaction.

Lastly, the importance of customer loyalty and building long-term relationships with consumers is emphasized by increasing competition and the ease with which consumers can compare prices and offers from different retailers. Loyalty programs, personalized discounts, and targeted communications are just a few of the strategies adopted to encourage repeat purchases and preference for a specific brand or retailer.

The complexity and multidimensionality of modern consumer behavior, therefore, require a holistic and multidisciplinary approach that integrates diverse skills and is capable of adapting quickly to market developments and emerging consumption habits.

In addition to what has been discussed, it is crucial to highlight how consumer behavior analysis must increasingly take into account cultural and demographic differences. Age, gender, cultural background, and socio-economic status diversity play a key role in shaping consumer preferences and expectations. For example, younger generations, such as Millennials and Generation Z, tend to be more sensitive to innovation and sustainability issues and have high expectations for personalization and the shopping experience.

Simultaneously, increased globalization and easy access to products and services from around the world have led to more demanding and informed consumers who seek quality and authenticity, willing to explore new options and product categories. This has made the market even more competitive and emphasized the need for companies to differentiate themselves and build a strong emotional connection with consumers.

Consumer psychology is another essential field of study to understand the motivations and buying drivers. Motivation theory, needs and desires dynamics, and studies on information processing and risk perception are all elements contributing to defining consumer behavior. A deep understanding of these aspects can help companies develop more effective marketing strategies and create products and services that genuinely meet consumers' needs and expectations.

Furthermore, the increasing importance of experiential marketing has led to a greater focus on the interaction between the consumer and the brand and the significance of creating memorable and engaging experiences. The concept of the "customer journey," the path consumers take from when they become aware of a product or service to purchase and beyond, has become central to marketing strategies. Analyzing and optimizing every touchpoint along this journey is essential for building lasting relationships with consumers and fostering loyalty and recommendations.

The analysis of social trends and changes in consumer lifestyles is another relevant aspect. Monitoring and anticipating these changes allows companies to adapt their products and services and to remain relevant in the market. For instance, the increased interest in a healthy and active lifestyle has led to the development of new market segments and opportunities for innovation in product categories such as food and beverages, clothing, and technology. Furthermore, the evolution of communication technologies and the increased use of mobile devices have led to new forms of interaction between consumers and brands. The ability to communicate in real-time and receive instant feedback offers unique engagement opportunities for companies and consumer listening, but also presents new challenges in terms of managing relationships and online reputation.

In conclusion, consumer behavior analysis is a continuously evolving field that requires a flexible and multifaceted approach, offering endless possibilities for learning and development for companies seeking to remain competitive and meet the needs of an increasingly informed and demanding consumer. An increasingly relevant aspect in consumer behavior analysis is the effect of sustainability and corporate social responsibility on purchasing decisions. Modern consumers are more informed and aware of environmental and social issues, and many studies have shown they are willing to pay more for products and services from ethical and sustainable companies. This has led businesses to implement greener practices and communicate their efforts in this direction to build a positive reputation and gain consumer trust.

The growth of e-commerce and social media has transformed the way consumers interact with brands and make purchasing decisions. The ability to read online reviews, compare prices and product features, and directly engage with companies through social platforms has empowered consumers, making them more informed. Consequently, companies must be increasingly transparent, responsive, and customer-oriented to build and maintain positive relationships with their target market.

In today's scenario, Big Data analysis and the use of artificial intelligence and machine learning techniques have become indispensable tools for understanding consumer behavior. Collecting and analyzing vast amounts of data enable companies to identify behavioral patterns, anticipate trends, and personalize offers to meet the specific needs of each individual. This level of personalization is crucial for creating satisfying shopping experiences and increasing customer retention.

The role of emotional branding is another key element in the current context. Emotions play a crucial role in purchasing decisions, and companies are increasingly aiming to build emotional connections with consumers through storytelling, design, advertising, and other marketing techniques. Creating a strong emotional bond can lead to greater customer loyalty and positive word-of-mouth, essential elements for the long-term success of a brand. Additionally, the importance of omnichannel experiences has grown exponentially. Modern consumers expect a seamless and consistent shopping experience across all channels, both online and offline. Therefore, companies must ensure an integrated and consistent presence across all touchpoints and ensure that the transition from one channel to another is as smooth and natural as possible.

Another relevant aspect is the evolution of consumer expectations regarding customer service. The speed and ease of access to information have led to increased expectations in terms of response times, availability, and service customization. Companies capable of providing excellent and proactive customer service can significantly differentiate themselves from the competition and gain consumer loyalty.

Lastly, but no less important, the increasing diversity and multiculturalism of modern societies demand an increasingly inclusive and adaptable approach. Understanding and respecting cultural, religious, and gender differences is essential for creating products and services that are welcoming and accessible to a diverse and global audience.

All these elements, combined with ongoing technological innovations and socio-cultural changes, make consumer behavior analysis a complex yet extremely stimulating field, offering virtually limitless opportunities for learning and growth.

In conclusion, consumer behavior analysis is a multidimensional and ever-evolving field that requires a holistic approach and adaptation to new trends and technologies. The growing consumer awareness of sustainability, ethics, and inclusivity is redefining the success parameters for companies and demands innovative, value-oriented strategies.

The rise of the digital age and the omnipresence of social media have strengthened consumer power, making it essential for companies to be transparent, responsive, and focused on building lasting relationships. The ability to leverage Big Data and artificial intelligence technologies to anticipate customer needs and personalize offerings has become a key factor in differentiation and competitiveness.

Emotional branding, omnichannel experiences, and excellent customer service are indispensable elements for meeting the rising expectations of consumers and building their loyalty. Additionally, embracing and respecting cultural, religious, and gender diversities are crucial for operating in a global and diverse market.

In summary, consumer behavior analysis is a strategic pillar guiding the development of effective products, services, and marketing campaigns. Companies that can interpret and anticipate the needs and desires of consumers, responding ethically and sustainably, are destined to thrive in an increasingly complex and dynamic market context. The depth and complexity of this field of study offer endless opportunities for learning and innovation, shaping the future of business and the relationship between brands and consumers.

13. Corporate Social Responsibility (Sustainability, Ethics, etc.)

Corporate Social Responsibility (CSR), also known as Responsabilità Sociale d'Impresa, represents a key concept in modern retail. It involves companies taking responsibility for the impact of their activities on the environment, society, and general well-being. This area comprises various dimensions, including environmental sustainability, business ethics, workers' rights, and community involvement.

Environmental sustainability is at the core of CSR practices. Retail companies commit to reducing ecological impact through optimized production processes, the use of sustainable and recyclable materials, waste management, CO_2 emission reduction, and energy conservation. These practices not only protect the environment but also build a positive brand image and satisfy the increasing consumer demand for environmentally responsible products and services.

Business ethics stands as another pillar of CSR. Ethical companies operate with integrity, transparency, and compliance with laws and regulations. They promote fair and safe working conditions, combat discrimination and child labor, and uphold human rights. Ethical conduct extends to the supply chain, selecting suppliers sharing responsible values and practices.

Community involvement is fundamental for responsible companies. Many retail companies develop volunteer programs, donations, sponsorships, and partnerships with non-profit organizations to support social, educational, and health-related causes. The goal is to contribute to the well-being of the communities they operate in and build positive relationships with various stakeholders.

Social inclusion and diversity are increasingly relevant themes in CSR. Companies strive to create inclusive work environments and promote diversity in terms of gender, ethnicity, sexual orientation, disabilities, and cultural backgrounds. This commitment is also reflected in product assortment, store accessibility, and advertising campaigns.

Furthermore, it's important to highlight that Corporate Social Responsibility is not just an ethical duty but also a competitive advantage. Companies adopting responsible practices tend to enjoy greater consumer loyalty, reduce reputational and legal risks, and attract talent motivated by ethical and sustainable values. In this context, CSR represents a strategic investment in the future of both the business and society at large.

Within the context of Corporate Social Responsibility, **transparency in relationships with consumers and stakeholders** is a crucial element. Companies must openly communicate their social and environmental initiatives and outcomes. Creating sustainability reports and certification by third-party entities are key tools to ensure authenticity and credibility in the actions undertaken. **Active involvement of employees** in CSR practices is another crucial element. Training, awareness, and employee inclusion in company decisions regarding sustainability can generate a positive work environment, increase productivity, and foster innovation. Companies prioritizing the well-being of their employees often make a significant difference in the landscape of Corporate Social Responsibility.

Another relevant aspect of CSR concerns the relationship with suppliers and the supply chain. Ethically responsible companies implement sustainable procurement policies, favoring suppliers adhering to high standards regarding human rights, working conditions, and environmental impact. Moreover, fair trade practices and the adoption of ethical and environmental certifications along the value chain contribute to ensuring responsible products and services.
CSR is also demonstrated through eco-design initiatives, aiming to reduce the environmental impact of products right from the design phase by considering the entire product lifecycle, from raw material extraction to the end of useful life. This approach promotes the use of

recycled and recyclable materials, energy consumption reduction, and waste minimization. **Waste management policies and recycling are fundamental components of companies' sustainability strategy**. Implementing differentiated waste collection systems, encouraging recycling, and reducing the use of non-biodegradable materials are concrete actions to limit the impact on the planet. Moreover, in the field of CSR, there has been a growing interest in gender issues and promoting equality. Companies are adopting gender equality policies, ensuring equal opportunities, pay equity, and representation at all organizational levels.

Consumer awareness and education play a fundamental role in promoting sustainability. Companies, through informative and ethical marketing campaigns, can influence consumer choices, directing them towards more responsible and conscious products and behaviors.

Finally, in the digital era, technology and social media play a crucial role in spreading CSR practices. Online presence allows companies to reach a wider audience and actively engage consumers in sustainability initiatives, creating a community of individuals committed and sensitive to social and environmental responsibility issues.

In discussions on Corporate Social Responsibility, **a significant factor is the investment in community and social development projects**. Many companies allocate a portion of their profits to projects related to education, health, and the well-being of local communities, thus aiming to contribute to the sustainable development of the areas in which they operate.

Collaboration with Non-Governmental Organizations (NGOs) and non-profit organizations is another method through which companies seek to maximize their positive impact. These partnerships can lead to the creation of joint projects and initiatives aimed at solving social, environmental, and developmental issues.

Furthermore, **ethical corporate governance** is a pillar of CSR. Responsible companies adopt transparent and inclusive governance models involving various stakeholders in the decision-making process. This helps prevent unethical behavior and promotes trust among the company, employees, customers, and investors.

Sustainable innovation is another relevant dimension of CSR. Companies are called to invest in research and development to create innovative products and services that reduce environmental impact and improve people's quality of life. Innovation can manifest in various ways, from introducing clean technologies to implementing new circular business models.

In the context of the climate crisis, the commitment of companies to reduce greenhouse gas emissions has become a central aspect of CSR. Many entrepreneurs are taking measures to reduce the carbon footprint of their activities through the use of renewable energies, energy efficiency, and emission offsetting.

Promoting diversity and inclusion in the workplace is another focal point of CSR. Creating an inclusive work environment that values differences and offers equal opportunities is essential to attract and retain talent and improve business performance.

Health and safety issues in the workplace are intrinsically linked to CSR. Ensuring a safe work environment, respectful of employees' health and well-being, is not only a legal obligation but also an ethical imperative reflecting the company's commitment to human rights protection.

Additionally, **attention to animal welfare has become an important component of**

CSR for companies in the food and cosmetics industry. Adopting ethical practices in animal management and choosing not to test products on animals are aspects that consumers increasingly consider in their purchasing decisions.

Another relevant aspect is the management of environmental and social risks. Responsible companies implement risk management systems that consider the social and environmental impacts of their activities to prevent and mitigate negative effects on society and the environment.

Lastly, it's crucial to emphasize the importance of involving customers in CSR. Listening to customers' needs and expectations and involving them in sustainability initiatives can strengthen the relationship between the company and the consumer, increasing customer loyalty and brand value.

Corporate Social Responsibility also extends to the ethical management of human resources, with companies adopting ethical and transparent hiring and personnel management practices, promoting continuous training, and professional development of employees.

An increasingly relevant dimension of CSR is transparency in business and

financial operations. This involves the preparation of accurate and honest corporate balance sheets and reports that reflect the company's financial and operational reality, contributing to building trust among stakeholders and preventing fraud and misconduct.

Supply chain traceability is another key element of CSR. Responsible companies actively work to ensure that their suppliers adhere to high standards in terms of human rights, working conditions, and environmental impact. This involves the implementation of monitoring and certification systems throughout the supply chain.

Commitment to combating corruption is fundamental. Companies must adopt rigorous policies and internal control systems to prevent, identify, and combat corruption in all its forms, both internally and externally to the company.

Companies are also called to actively engage in dialogue with policymakers and regulators to contribute to the development of regulations and policies that promote sustainability and social responsibility, thus demonstrating a proactive commitment to building a fair and sustainable regulatory framework.

Additionally, creating a positive and stimulating work environment is a crucial aspect of CSR. Companies can implement various strategies, such as introducing corporate welfare programs, promoting work-life balance, and creating inclusive and welcoming workspaces.

Engagement with stakeholders and dialogue are fundamental to identify and address the expectations and concerns of all those affected by the company's activities. This engagement can lead to more informed and sustainable decisions and contribute to building long-term relationships based on trust and collaboration.

Environmental education and awareness are also important tools for CSR. Companies can play a key role in educating consumers and stakeholders about sustainability issues, promoting responsible and conscious behaviors.

Finally, responsible waste management and the circular economy are increasingly central themes. Companies are called to reduce waste production, promote recycling and material reuse, and implement business models that value resources and reduce environmental impact.

Throughout all this, it's essential that companies effectively and transparently communicate their efforts and results in terms of CSR, using various platforms and communication channels to reach a broad and diversified audience.

In conclusion, Corporate Social Responsibility (CSR) is a multidimensional concept that requires deep and continuous commitment from companies in multiple areas. From environmental sustainability to ethical human resource management, from financial transparency to the fight against corruption, every aspect of CSR contributes to building a company that operates in respect of the society and the environment in which it operates.

Supply chain traceability and ethical supplier selection are fundamental to ensure the company's commitment is consistent across the entire value chain. This not only mitigates the risks associated with irresponsible practices but also contributes to building a strong and reputable brand, reinforcing stakeholder trust.

Active engagement in dialogue with policymakers and regulatory bodies is also crucial. Contributing to the development of regulations promoting sustainability and social equity is a significant part of engaging in a

responsible and proactive manner in societal
development.

14. Human Resources Management

Human resources management is a critical
component in the modern retail industry. It
serves as the pillar supporting operational
efficiency, employee satisfaction, and
consequently, customer satisfaction. It
encompasses various subcategories and
practices, including personnel selection, training
and development, performance management,
compensation and benefits, and the maintenance
of a positive and inclusive work environment.

1. **Personnel Selection**: Accurate personnel
   selection is fundamental. Retail requires a variety
   of skills, from supply chain management to retail
   sales. Attracting and selecting individuals with
   the right skills and attitude is essential for a
   company's success.
2. **Training and Development**: Investing in
   employee training and development is crucial.
   This not only improves employee skills but also

increases productivity, service quality, and innovation within the company.

3. **Performance Management**: Monitoring and evaluating employee performance is essential to ensure that quality standards are maintained and to identify areas for improvement. Setting clear and realistic goals, coupled with constructive feedback, helps motivate employees.

4. **Compensation and Benefits**: Offering competitive compensation and attractive benefits is crucial for attracting and retaining top talent. This includes not only salary but also bonuses, insurance, wellness programs, and other incentives.

5. **Positive and Inclusive Work Environment**: Creating a work environment that promotes diversity, inclusion, and respect is essential. A positive work climate contributes to employee well-being, reduces turnover, and increases productivity.

6. **Workplace Safety**: Ensuring workplace safety is an absolute priority. Implementing and maintaining high health and safety standards reduces the risk of injuries and absences, improving worker satisfaction and the company's reputation.

7. **Communication and Engagement**: Effective communication and employee engagement are central to human resources management.

Keeping employees informed and involved in company decisions increases their sense of belonging and motivation.

8. **Regulations and Compliance**: Adhering to local, national, and international labor rights regulations is crucial. Compliance helps prevent disputes, fines, and damage to the company's reputation.

In conclusion, effective human resources management is essential for the success and sustainability of retail businesses. Through ethical and innovative practices, it's possible to create a work environment that values and supports employees, contributing to the company's long-term success.

Human resources management in retail can also be influenced by the adoption of innovative technologies, such as advanced human resources management software, enabling better resource planning, performance analysis, and talent management. Implementing such technological tools can significantly contribute to operational efficiency and achieving corporate objectives.

Moreover, human resources management must adapt to emerging and continuously evolving market challenges. For instance, the increasing emphasis on work-life balance, employee well-being, and environmental sustainability has become crucial factors that companies must consider in personnel management. In this context, flexible policies, such as remote work or flexible hours, are increasingly important to meet employee needs and expectations.

Inoltre, la crescente diversità delle forze lavoro richiede una gestione inclusiva e multiculturale.

Human Resource Management in Retail: Enhancing Workforce Dynamics

Companies must implement anti-discrimination policies, promote diversity, and ensure that all employees have equal opportunities for growth and development. Diversity and inclusion training can help build a corporate culture that embraces and values differences.

Change Management in Retail Industry

Change management is another area requiring attention in human resource management. Retail sector companies must be ready to adapt quickly to market changes, new business models, and technological innovations. This involves developing skills and adaptability among employees and creating a corporate culture that encourages innovation and continuous learning.

Career Management and Succession Planning

Career management and succession planning are key elements in retail human resource management. Offering clear career paths and development opportunities helps retain talent within the organization, ensuring long-term business continuity. Succession planning is particularly crucial for key roles where experience and skills are vital for business success.

Employee Motivation Strategies

Employee motivation is another fundamental aspect. Incentive strategies such as performance bonuses, recognition, and non-monetary incentives play a significant role in maintaining high morale and employee engagement.

Active Listening and Continuous Feedback

Active listening and constant feedback are essential tools to understand employees' needs, expectations, and concerns. Through employee satisfaction surveys, listening sessions, and open feedback channels, companies can gather valuable insights and act accordingly to improve the work environment and human resource management.

Training and Development in Retail

In the context of retail, addressing training and staff development is essential. Companies are increasingly investing in training programs that allow employees to acquire new skills, stay updated on industry trends, and adapt to market changes. Continuous training is particularly important in an industry where technological innovation and consumer expectations are constantly evolving.

Workplace Health and Safety

Ensuring workplace health and safety is crucial. Companies must ensure employees operate in a safe and healthy environment, minimizing the risks of injuries and occupational illnesses. This involves not only complying with health and safety regulations but also investing in safety training, personal protective equipment, and continuous improvements in working conditions.

Managing Seasonal Peaks and Demand Fluctuations

Effective management of seasonal peaks and demand variations in retail requires flexible and scalable workforce planning. Handling temporary resources, fixed-term contracts, and overtime work is essential to efficiently meet customer needs while maintaining employee well-being.

Employee Engagement and Conflict Management

Employee engagement is central, as motivated and engaged employees are more productive and contribute to a positive work environment. Initiatives like team building, corporate events, and recognition programs can strengthen a sense of belonging and enhance employee satisfaction and retention.

Internal Conflict Management

Addressing internal conflicts is crucial in the diverse roles and responsibilities within the retail sector. Effective policies and procedures for conflict resolution are essential to promote a harmonious and cooperative work environment.

Internal Communication and Performance Management

Internal communication is a key element to ensure that all employees are informed and engaged in company decisions. An effective communication system contributes to creating a sense of unity and belonging, improves transparency, and helps prevent misunderstandings and frustrations.

Diversity and Inclusion in Human Resource Management

Diversity and inclusivity are pivotal elements in human resource management in retail. Progressive companies are implementing inclusion policies aiming to create a welcoming and supportive work environment for all, regardless of gender, ethnicity, sexual orientation, age, or disability. Promoting diversity is not only ethically right but can also lead to greater innovation and a better understanding of diverse customer segments.

Employee Well-being and Compensation

Employee well-being has become increasingly central. Corporate welfare programs, psychological support services, and initiatives to balance work and personal life have become fundamental elements of human resource management strategy. These services help reduce stress, increase job satisfaction, and subsequently decrease employee turnover.

Compensation and Benefits

The structuring of competitive remuneration packages, including not only the base salary but also bonuses, incentives, non-monetary benefits, and opportunities for professional growth, is crucial to attract and retain talent in the retail sector. A fair and transparent remuneration policy also contributes to creating a climate of equity and employee satisfaction.

Advanced HR Technologies and Work Sustainability

The adoption of advanced technologies in human resource management is transforming how companies interact with their employees. Cloud-based Human Resource Management (HRM) systems, e-learning platforms, digital recruiting solutions, and data analytics tools are becoming essential for effective personnel management. These technologies simplify and optimize HR processes, improve communication and employee engagement, and support data-driven decision-making.

Work Sustainability and Career Management

The sustainability of work in terms of hours, workload, and conditions is an increasingly relevant issue. Seeking a balance between company needs and workers' rights is a constant challenge. Introducing flexible work models, telecommuting, and initiatives for employee health are examples of how companies are trying to make work more sustainable and adaptable to individual needs.

Career Management and Succession Planning

Managing careers and succession planning are key elements to ensure business continuity and talent development. Identifying and training future leaders, managing internal mobility, and offering clear and motivating career paths are fundamental strategies to ensure long-term growth and success.

Continuous Training and Employee Engagement

Continuous training is an indispensable element in human resource management. Retail companies significantly invest in training and development programs to enhance their employees' skills. This can involve both technical skills and soft skills such as leadership, communication, and time management. The goal is to prepare employees to handle the challenges of the ever-evolving market and adapt to changing consumer needs.

Employee Engagement

Similarly, employee engagement is crucial. Companies that establish a positive and motivating work environment are more likely to maintain high levels of productivity and low turnover rates. Creating an environment that values employees' opinions and involves them in decision-making processes contributes to improving morale and emotional investment in the company's success.

Challenges in Human Resource Management in Retail

Seasonal Staff Management

Human resource management in retail faces the challenge of managing seasonal personnel. During demand peaks such as holidays or seasonal sales, hiring additional staff and ensuring their adequate training and integration is essential. This requires careful planning and efficient resource management to avoid staff shortages or additional costs.

Performance Evaluation and Constructive Feedback

Performance evaluation and constructive feedback are other crucial aspects. An effective evaluation system helps employees understand company expectations, receive recognition for their achievements, and identify areas for improvement. Regular and constructive feedback is vital for professional development and employee satisfaction.

Work-Life Balance

Balancing work and personal life is another area of focus. Retail companies are seeking innovative solutions to offer flexible working hours, remote work options, and support for managing family responsibilities. The goal is to create a balanced work environment that promotes employee health and well-being.

Labor Legislation and Compliance

Attention to labor laws and regulatory compliance is essential. Companies must stay updated on all labor laws and regulations concerning workers' rights, workplace safety, and pay equality. Compliance with these regulations is not only mandatory but also contributes to building a positive reputation and prevents potential sanctions and legal disputes.

Human Resource Management in Retail: A Complex Landscape

Human resource management in retail is a complex mosaic of interconnected and interdependent processes, policies, and practices. This dynamic and challenging sector requires careful and targeted attention to its human capital, as employee satisfaction, efficiency, and productivity directly impact overall company performance and the customer experience.

Continuous Training: A Cornerstone

Continuous training emerges as one of the pillars of this management, being crucial not only to equip personnel with necessary skills but also to ensure the company maintains a competitive edge in an ever-evolving market. Training isn't just an investment in the present; it represents a commitment to the company's future, ensuring it's always prepared to address new challenges and opportunities.

Employee Engagement and Positive Work Environment

Employee engagement and creating a positive work environment are not only ethical aspirations but strategic necessities. A motivated and engaged employee often equates to a productive and loyal one, reducing turnover costs and enhancing the quality of customer service.

The Challenge of Seasonal Staff Management, Performance Evaluation, Work-Life Balance, and Regulatory Compliance

These aspects are all crucial cogs in a well-oiled machine that a company must manage effectively and prudently. Non-compliance or inadequate management of any of these aspects can lead to inefficiencies, legal problems, or reputational damage, with potentially severe repercussions for the business.

Conclusion: Strategic Human Resource Management in Retail

Human resource management in the retail sector isn't just administrative task execution; it's a strategic function that requires vision, foresight, and adaptability. Its effectiveness significantly determines the company's success, as people, with their skills, energy, and passions, are the true drivers of every business activity. Ensuring they are well managed, motivated, and satisfied is not just an ethical duty but a winning strategic choice.

15. Supplier Relations

Supplier relations represent a fundamental aspect in the value chain of retail. In an increasingly competitive and globalized market, effectively managing these relations is crucial to ensure product quality, operational efficiency, and cost sustainability. Strategies and practices adopted in this domain can significantly impact a company's success.

Selecting the Right Partners

One of the primary challenges in managing supplier relations is selecting the right partners. It's crucial to identify suppliers who not only offer high-quality products at competitive prices but also share the company's values and goals. Additionally, verifying suppliers' financial stability, reliability, and reputation is fundamental to minimize risks associated with delays, non-deliveries, or quality issues.

Contract Negotiation

Contract negotiation is another key element in supplier relations. Contractual conditions, such as prices, payment terms, service levels, and penalty clauses, must be carefully defined to balance the needs of the company and the supplier while ensuring flexibility and adaptability to market changes.

Performance Management

Another significant aspect is managing supplier performance. Constantly monitoring product quality, delivery times, and service levels is essential to identify any issues and intervene promptly. Implementing evaluation systems and feedback can enhance transparency and communication between parties, fostering the creation of strong, long-term relationships.

Sustainability and Ethics

Additionally, sustainability and ethics play an increasingly important role in supplier relations. Companies are more attentive in selecting partners adopting environmentally responsible, socially conscious, and labor-friendly practices. Promoting sustainable practices in the supply chain can not only enhance the company's image and reputation but also reduce risks associated with regulatory violations or scandals.

Technological Innovation and Digitalization

Finally, technological innovation and digitalization are transforming supplier relationship management. Adopting digital platforms, blockchain, and big data solutions can improve the efficiency, transparency, and traceability of transactions, fostering collaboration and information sharing between the company and its suppliers.

In summary, supplier relations are a critical element for retail, requiring careful and strategic management. Selecting the right partners, effectively negotiating contracts, monitoring performance, emphasizing sustainability, and adopting innovative technologies are all factors contributing to building successful relationships that generate value for the company and the entire value chain.

Proactive Relationship Management

In the context of supplier relations, a proactive approach to relationship management is essential. Establishing open and regular communication can help prevent misunderstandings and swiftly resolve any disputes. Seminars, meetings, and workshops can be useful tools to strengthen mutual understanding and share best practices, promoting a partnership rather than a mere business transaction.

Risk Management

Another important issue is risk management. Companies must adopt approaches and tools to identify, assess, and mitigate risks associated with suppliers, such as dependence on a single supplier, raw material price volatility, geopolitical risks, and risks related to climate change. Effective risk management can reduce uncertainty and ensure operational continuity.

Value Co-Creation and Skills Development

The concept of value co-creation is also relevant in the context of supplier relations. This approach involves close collaboration between the company and suppliers to identify and leverage opportunities to create added value for both parties. Through value co-creation, companies and suppliers can develop innovative solutions, improve efficiency and quality, and more effectively respond to market and consumer needs.

Furthermore, the importance of training and skill development for both the company and suppliers is worth considering. Investing in training and development programs can enhance human resources skills and capabilities, fostering innovation and operational efficiency. Moreover, training can be a key tool in promoting a culture of sustainability and social responsibility within the supply chain.

Additionally, the adoption of Lean Management tools and practices can optimize processes and reduce waste, fostering greater efficiency and competitiveness. Implementing Lean principles can positively influence not only production but also logistics, quality, customer service, and other aspects of business operations.

Finally, Flexibility and Adaptability

Flexibility and adaptability are fundamental skills to effectively manage supplier relations in an ever-evolving business environment. The ability to quickly adapt to market changes, new consumer trends, and competitive challenges can make the difference between success and failure. Organizational agility and a culture of continuous learning are key factors in this context.

In summary, supplier relations management in retail requires a holistic approach that takes into account various factors such as communication, risk management, value co-creation, training, adoption of Lean practices, and organizational flexibility. Only through careful consideration of all these elements can companies hope to build lasting and fruitful relationships with their suppliers.

Continuous Supplier Performance Evaluation

Moreover, it's crucial for retail companies to constantly examine and evaluate supplier performance. Implementing an effective performance evaluation system can help identify areas for improvement, incentivize suppliers to raise their standards, and ensure that the company's expectations are met. This process may involve analyzing various Key Performance Indicators (KPIs) such as delivery punctuality, product quality, customer service levels, and responsiveness to change requests.

Sustainability in Supplier Relations

Sustainability is becoming an increasingly relevant consideration in supplier relations. Companies are often required to demonstrate their commitment to sustainable and responsible practices, which involves selecting suppliers who adhere to these values. Environmental certifications, codes of conduct, and audit programs can be useful tools to verify and ensure suppliers' compliance with sustainability principles.

Technology's Role in Supplier Management

The importance of technology in supplier relations management cannot be underestimated. Adopting advanced technological solutions like Enterprise Resource Planning (ERP) systems, e-procurement platforms, and blockchain-based solutions can simplify and optimize the supplier management process. These technologies can enhance transaction transparency, efficiency, accuracy, reduce lead times, and improve collaboration between companies and suppliers.

Diversification of Suppliers and Negotiation Strategies

In a globalized landscape, supplier diversification is an additional strategy to reduce reliance on a single supplier and mitigate risks associated with supply chain disruptions. Having a variety of suppliers across different geographical regions can help companies navigate crises better, such as logistic disruptions, currency fluctuations, and political instability.

Furthermore, the ability to negotiate favorable terms and conditions is an essential aspect of supplier management. Companies must negotiate prices, payment terms, delivery conditions, and other key factors to ensure maximum flexibility and minimize costs. Training staff in effective negotiation techniques and using cost analysis tools can be very helpful in this context.

Contract Management and Trust Building

Another focal point is contract management. A well-drafted contract that clearly details expectations, responsibilities, and legal implications for both parties is fundamental in preventing future disputes. Contract management involves not only drafting and negotiation but also monitoring compliance and managing contractual changes.

Finally, trust and integrity are at the core of any successful business relationship. Building trust relationships with suppliers can lead to increased collaboration, shared innovation, and solutions to common problems. Trust is built through consistency, open communication, fair conflict resolution, and mutual respect for commitments.

Continuous Engagement and Long-Term Collaboration

Continuing the exploration of supplier relations, emphasizing engagement and long-term collaboration is fundamental. Companies seeking enduring and mutually beneficial relationships with suppliers can foster an environment of growth and shared innovation. This might involve sharing market trends, consumer feedback, and product development strategies, contributing to the creation of better and more competitive products and services.

Risk Management in Supplier Relations

Risk management is another crucial element in supplier relationship management. Companies must identify, evaluate, and mitigate potential risks associated with their suppliers, which might include financial stability, operational risks, reputation risks, and legal risks. Implementing risk management tools and processes, such as due diligence, risk assessments, and contingency plans, can help companies protect themselves from unforeseen events and ensure operational continuity.

Flexibility and Adaptability

Similarly, flexibility and adaptability are essential in a continuously changing business environment. The ability to quickly adapt to market demand fluctuations, changes in raw materials, and cost fluctuations can be a determining factor for success. Companies and suppliers must work together to develop strategies and solutions that enable them to effectively address these challenges while maintaining quality and efficiency.

Training and Skill Development

The importance of training and skill development cannot be overlooked. Providing employees with the skills and knowledge necessary to effectively manage supplier relations can lead to better-informed decisions, improved negotiation, and overall higher satisfaction. Training could cover areas such as communication, negotiation, conflict resolution, data analysis, and project management.

Regulatory Compliance and Industry Standards

Attention to regulations and industry standards is equally essential. Compliance with local, national, and international laws, as well as quality and safety standards, is crucial to avoid penalties, reputation damage, and potential legal actions. Maintaining an open and proactive dialogue with suppliers regarding compliance expectations can help prevent misunderstandings and ensure alignment on goals and standards.

Supplier Involvement in Planning and Strategic Innovation

Finally, involving suppliers in planning and strategic innovation can lead to a competitive advantage. Inviting suppliers to participate in brainstorming sessions, workshops, and research and development projects can stimulate new ideas, innovative solutions, and continuous improvements. This collaboration strengthens partnerships and creates a sense of involvement and belonging, contributing to the mutual success of companies and suppliers.

Sustainability in Supplier Relations

Sustainability is another crucial aspect when discussing supplier relations. Many companies are currently assessing their suppliers' ecological footprint, considering factors such as resource usage, carbon emissions, and ethical work practices. Collaborating with sustainable suppliers not only enhances a company's image but also contributes to reducing environmental and social risks throughout the supply chain. Commitment to sustainability can also lead to innovation, the creation of eco-friendly products, and new market opportunities.

The Importance of Transparency in Supplier Relations

The importance of transparency in supplier relations is another element that deserves attention. Transparency allows both parties to have access to clear and accurate information, thus reducing the risk of misunderstandings and conflicts. It's also essential to build and maintain trust, a key element in any business relationship. Companies need to promote open and honest communication, sharing expectations, feedback, and concerns constructively.

Role of Technology in Supplier Management

Technology plays an increasingly central role in managing supplier relations. The use of digital platforms and technological tools can enhance the efficiency, accuracy, and speed of transactions. For instance, Enterprise Resource Planning (ERP) systems and e-procurement platforms can streamline the purchasing process, while big data solutions and analytics can provide valuable insights into supplier performance and aid in identifying areas for improvement.

Supplier Diversification and Performance Measurement

Supplier diversification is another strategy that companies can adopt to mitigate procurement-associated risks. Having a variety of suppliers ensures that a company is not overly dependent on a single supplier, thus reducing vulnerability to supply chain interruptions, price variations, and other issues. Diversification can also offer access to a broader range of skills, technologies, and innovations. At the same time, measuring supplier performance through Key Performance

Indicators (KPIs) and regular evaluations is essential to ensure that suppliers meet required standards. Performance analysis can reveal areas where suppliers can improve, contributing to the growth and development of both parties.

Ethics and Corporate Social Responsibility

Finally, ethics and corporate social responsibility must not be undervalued. Companies need to ensure that their suppliers respect workers' rights, environmental regulations, and ethical standards. This not only improves the company's reputation but also helps create a fair and sustainable work environment throughout the entire supply chain.

In Conclusion

Effectively managing supplier relations is crucial for the success of a retail business. This requires a holistic approach considering various key factors like negotiation, sustainability, transparency, technological innovation, diversification, performance evaluation, and corporate ethics. Adopting sustainable and ethical practices is essential to build strong and lasting relationships with suppliers. This not only helps protect the environment and ensure workers' rights but also improves the company's image and provides access to new market opportunities. Therefore, it's essential for companies to assess the suppliers' ecological footprint and actively promote ethical work practices. Transparency, open communication, technology, diversification, and regular evaluation of supplier performance are vital strategies to mitigate risks and ensure quality. In summary, managing supplier relations is a complex process that requires constant attention to various aspects. Companies that adopt an ethical, transparent, technologically advanced, and strategic approach are more likely to build lasting relationships with suppliers, gaining competitive advantages, and contributing to a fairer and sustainable economy.

16. Regulations and Compliance

Managing regulations and compliance is fundamental in the retail sector, as businesses must operate in accordance with a wide range of laws and regulations at the local, national, and international levels. These can cover various areas such as product safety, consumer protection, ethical business practices, the environment, health and safety at work, data protection, labels, and more.

First and foremost, it's essential for retail companies to be aware of the laws and regulations applicable to their business. This requires in-depth research and continuous monitoring of legislative changes since non-compliance can result in severe penalties, reputation damage, and financial losses. A profound knowledge of legislation also enables companies to identify opportunities to gain a competitive advantage, such as accessing tax incentives or funding for sustainability.

Once relevant regulations are identified, companies must implement processes and procedures to ensure compliance. This can include staff training, creating operational manuals, adopting quality management systems, implementing technologies for product monitoring and traceability, and conducting regular audits.

Another crucial aspect is managing relationships with regulatory authorities. Companies must be able to effectively communicate with regulatory bodies, understand regulatory requirements, and promptly respond to requests for information or inspections. Furthermore, a good relationship with authorities can facilitate access to useful information and resources, contributing to building a positive reputation in the industry.

Finally, transparency and communication are fundamental. Companies must clearly inform consumers, business partners, and other stakeholders about their commitments and actions for regulatory compliance. This contributes to building trust and credibility while mitigating the risks of legal disputes and damage to the company's image.

In summary, managing regulations and compliance in the retail sector is a complex and ever-evolving task that requires constant commitment and a well-defined strategy. Companies that effectively fulfill these responsibilities not only avoid risks and penalties but can also strengthen their market position and create long-term value.

In the Context of Regulations and Compliance

Within the realm of regulations and compliance, retail companies must pay particular attention to the realm of data protection. With the advent of GDPR in Europe and similar laws in other parts of the world, managing customer data has become a crucial issue. Companies must ensure that personal data is collected, processed, stored, and destroyed in accordance with the law, and they must be prepared to respond to data subject requests regarding access, rectification, or deletion of their information.

Furthermore, food safety is another relevant aspect for retailers, especially those operating in the food sector. Regulations in this field are extremely stringent and require companies to implement rigorous quality control systems, supply chain traceability, accurate food labeling, and product recall management. Non-compliance in this sector can have serious consequences not only in terms of penalties but also for public health and corporate reputation. Product labeling is also subject to specific regulations, varying depending on the product type and the country of sale. Companies must ensure that product labels contain all information required by law, such as composition, usage instructions, safety warnings, and environmental information. Misleading or incorrect labeling can lead to penalties and damage consumer trust.

Environmental Sustainability

Environmental sustainability is another area where regulations are becoming increasingly stringent. Companies are encouraged, if not obligated, to adopt eco-friendly practices, reduce the environmental impact of their operations, and promote responsible consumption. This includes waste management, efficient resource use, reducing greenhouse gas emissions, and adopting eco-friendly packaging.

To tackle all these challenges, many retail companies are investing in advanced technologies such as blockchain, artificial intelligence, and the Internet of Things. These can help monitor and ensure regulatory compliance more efficiently and effectively. Adopting these technologies can also offer competitive advantages by improving operational efficiency, product traceability, customized offerings, and customer loyalty.

Furthermore, companies must also consider regulations related to workers' rights and labor conditions. It's essential that employees' rights are respected, work conditions are safe and healthy, and fair and inclusive policies are adopted. Ethical human resource management is not only a legal obligation but also contributes to creating a positive work environment, attracting and retaining talent, and improving the company's image.

Finally, issues related to intellectual property, such as trademarks, patents, and copyrights, are also of great importance in the retail sector. Protecting intellectual property is essential to preserve a company's identity and competitiveness, while respecting others' rights is crucial to avoid legal disputes and reputational damage.

In summary, managing regulations and compliance in the retail sector is a multidimensional task that requires careful planning, the implementation of suitable systems and procedures, and continuous staff training.

The ability to navigate effectively through this intricate regulatory landscape can make the difference between success and failure in today's competitive retail market.

Within the Realm of Regulations and Compliance

In managing regulations and compliance, retail companies must also pay attention to local and international norms concerning the import and export of goods. These rules can involve customs duties, import restrictions on certain products, and safety and quality standards that goods must meet. Knowledge and adherence to these rules are crucial to avoid delays, additional costs, and potential legal sanctions.

Another significant aspect concerns the advertising and promotion of products. Advertising laws vary considerably from one country to another but generally prohibit misleading or deceptive advertising and mandate the disclosure of certain product information in advertisements. Retail companies must be particularly attentive in creating and disseminating advertising material to comply with regulations and maintain consumer trust. Additionally, competition laws are another crucial element in managing retail activities. These laws are designed to promote competition and prevent unfair or anti-competitive business practices. Companies must be aware of restrictions on price-fixing, exclusive agreements, and abuses of dominant positions, acting proactively to ensure compliance and prevent potential sanctions.

The rapidly growing e-commerce sector presents additional challenges in terms of regulatory compliance. Online retail companies must deal with issues related to online consumer protection, cross-border transactions, digital taxation, and cybersecurity. Effectively managing these aspects is essential to maintain customer trust, minimize legal and operational risks, and ensure the long-term sustainability of online business.

Accessibility and Social Responsibility

Another crucial consideration is accessibility. Many countries impose specific regulations to ensure that retail stores and services are accessible to people with disabilities. This may include adjusting physical structures, providing assistance services, and adapting websites and apps to ensure digital accessibility. Complying with these regulations is not only a legal requirement but also an opportunity to expand the customer base and improve the company's image.

Moreover, the growing attention to human rights and corporate social responsibility has led to the introduction of regulations requiring companies to monitor and account for the social and environmental impact of their supply chains. Companies must take measures to prevent and mitigate the risks of human rights violations, labor exploitation, and environmental damage in their operations and value chains.

In summary, the regulatory landscape in the retail sector is extremely complex and dynamic, requiring companies to maintain constant vigilance and adapt to new challenges and opportunities. Regulatory compliance is not just a matter of law enforcement but is integrated into business strategy, risk management, and value creation for the company and its stakeholders.

Managing Regulatory Compliance

Managing regulations and compliance in the retail sector is a crucial aspect that impacts every element of business operations. The complexity of the rules requires a proactive and informed approach to navigate effectively through challenges and ensure the sustainability and compliance of the enterprise.

An essential component in this context is continuous training and updating of company personnel on legislation and norms. Knowledge of laws at the local, national, and international levels is crucial to avoid possible infractions and sanctions. Additionally, staff training contributes to building a corporate culture based on regulatory compliance and integrity, a key element in establishing and maintaining consumer and stakeholder trust.

An effective strategy for managing regulations also involves implementing internal monitoring and control systems. These systems help identify potential non-compliance risks promptly and take corrective measures, minimizing the negative impact on the company. In this context, the use of advanced technologies and digital solutions can significantly enhance the effectiveness of control processes and ensure greater transparency and accountability.

Beyond compliance with regulations, retail companies must consider the impact of their decisions on local communities and society in general. Corporate social responsibility and environmental sustainability have become central aspects in evaluating corporate performance. Compliance with environmental, social, and governance (ESG) regulations can not only mitigate risks but also create differentiation and competitive advantage in the market.

Finally, continuous communication and dialogue with regulatory authorities, industry associations, and other stakeholders are essential to anticipate and understand changes in the regulatory landscape. Active participation in discussions, technical panels, and industry initiatives can facilitate the company's adaptation to new regulations and influence the development of more balanced and sustainable norms.

In conclusion, managing regulations and compliance in the retail sector is a complex and multifaceted process that requires specific skills, ongoing attention, and a strategic vision. A company's ability to successfully navigate this dynamic regulatory environment will significantly determine its resilience, reputation, and its capacity to create long-term value for shareholders, customers, and society as a whole.

17. Internationalization and Globalization

Internationalization and globalization are essential strategies for the expansion of retail companies in foreign markets. Through these processes, companies can access new customers, diversify risks associated with specific markets, and take advantage of economies of scale. However, various challenges must be addressed, and several aspects must be considered to succeed in this endeavor.

1. **Market Analysis:** Companies must conduct in-depth analysis of target markets. This includes understanding consumer preferences, economic conditions, competition, and local regulations. SWOT analysis (Strengths, Weaknesses, Opportunities, Threats) can help evaluate opportunities and risks associated with specific international markets.

2. **Cultural Adaptation:** Cultural sensitivity and adaptation are crucial for international success. Companies must personalize their products, services, and marketing strategies to meet the needs and expectations of local consumers. Understanding cultural differences can also help build positive relationships with suppliers, business partners, and local employees.

3. **Entry Strategies:** Various modes of entry into international markets exist, such as exportation, joint ventures, strategic alliances, franchising, and foreign-owned subsidiaries. The choice of entry mode depends on factors like available resources, desired control level, and the risk tolerance of the company.

4. **Supply Chain and Logistics:** International expansion requires effective management of the supply chain and logistics. Companies must consider factors such as transportation costs, customs duties, import/export regulations, and inventory management. Adopting advanced technologies can help optimize logistics and reduce costs.

5. **Regulations and Compliance:** Companies must navigate the complex regulatory framework of foreign markets. This includes compliance with local laws, adaptation to environmental and labor regulations, and tax management. Regulatory compliance is essential to avoid sanctions and protect the company's reputation.

6. **Branding and Communication:** A strong brand and effective communication are essential to build trust and attract customers in new markets. Branding strategies must be adapted to local cultural characteristics and consumer behaviors, while communication channels must be selected based on their penetration and relevance in the target market.

7. **Personnel Management:** Internationalization requires managing diverse teams and understanding local work practices. Cross-cultural training, adaptation of human resource policies, and promoting an inclusive work

environment are essential to motivate employees and foster collaboration.

8. **Sustainability and Social Responsibility:** Companies must demonstrate commitment to sustainability and social responsibility, especially in foreign markets. Adhering to environmental regulations, adopting ethical practices, and engaging with local communities can enhance the company's image and contribute to its global success.

In summary, internationalization and globalization in the retail sector require strategic planning, cultural adaptation, and careful management of various operational aspects. Companies that successfully navigate this context can access new growth opportunities, strengthen their competitive position, and increase their resilience in the face of global market challenges. **Risk and Opportunity Assessment:** Before internationalizing, retail companies must conduct a thorough evaluation of risks and opportunities. This includes analyzing political stability, exchange rates, inflation levels, and economic growth in target markets. Companies must be prepared to quickly adapt to evolving market conditions and mitigate risks through appropriate strategies. 9. **Research and Development:** Investing in research and development (R&D) can help companies innovate and adapt their products and services to the specific needs of international consumers. R&D can lead to greater product differentiation, offering a competitive advantage in global markets.

9. Stakeholder Relations: Building strong relationships with local stakeholders, including customers, suppliers, governments, and business partners, is fundamental. Open and constructive dialogue can contribute to creating a favorable business environment and resolving any conflicts promptly.

10. Language Skills Development: The ability to communicate effectively in various languages is a fundamental asset for companies operating globally. Employee language training and hiring multilingual staff can facilitate communication and improve mutual understanding.

11. Financial Management: Internationalization involves financial challenges such as managing cash flows in different currencies, optimizing capital structure, and mitigating financial risks. Effective financial strategies are crucial to support international growth and ensure the company's financial stability.

12. Adaptation of Distribution Channels: Companies must adapt and optimize their distribution channels based on local infrastructure, regulations, and consumer preferences. Selecting reliable distributors and effectively using online and offline channels can improve market coverage and customer satisfaction.

13. Digitalization and Technology: Adopting digital technologies can help companies optimize operations, improve customer interaction, and collect valuable data. E-commerce platforms, Customer Relationship Management (CRM) systems, and data analytics solutions are essential tools for successful global competition.

14. Data Analysis and Market Intelligence: Effective use of data analysis and market intelligence can provide valuable insights into market trends, consumer behavior, and competitor performance. This information can guide the company in making strategic decisions and adapting product and service offerings.

15. Global Marketing Strategies: Developing and implementing effective global marketing strategies is crucial. This may include multichannel advertising campaigns, localized promotional events, and content marketing strategies tailored to diverse cultures and demographic groups.

These points highlight the complexity and multidimensionality of the internationalization and globalization process in the retail sector. Companies must consider a wide range of factors and adopt a flexible and proactive approach to successfully navigate international markets.

18. Positioning Strategies: Defining a clear positioning strategy is crucial to create a strong and distinctive brand identity on an international level. This involves understanding how the brand is perceived in different markets and adapting brand communication to resonate with local cultures.

19. Local Regulations and Compliance: Companies must ensure compliance with local regulations, which can vary significantly from one country to another. This includes labor laws, trade standards, environmental regulations, and tax requirements. Knowledge of and adherence to these regulations are crucial to avoid legal sanctions and reputational damage.

20. Collaborations and Partnerships: Establishing collaborations and partnerships with local entities can be an effective strategy to accelerate international expansion. This may include joint ventures, strategic alliances, franchising, and licensing agreements, offering access to local resources, skills, and distribution networks.

21. Supply Chain Management: Optimizing the global supply chain is a fundamental challenge. This includes managing suppliers, logistics, production, and distribution efficiently and sustainably, considering regional differences in infrastructure, costs, and regulations.

22. Customer Experience and Service:

Offering exceptional customer experience and high-quality customer service is crucial in every market. Adapting customer support services to languages, time zones, and local expectations can increase customer satisfaction and brand loyalty.

23. Staff Training and Development:

Training and developing staff are essential to build a competent and motivated team. Companies must invest in specific training programs that prepare employees for the challenges and opportunities of globalization.

24. Market Analysis and Segmentation:

Conducting detailed market analysis and defining clear customer segments are essential steps to develop effective marketing and sales strategies. Understanding the needs, preferences, and purchasing behaviors of local consumers can help personalize offerings and successfully position the brand.

18. Social Responsibility and Sustainability:

Global companies must take responsibility for their social and environmental impacts. Implementing sustainable practices, promoting corporate ethics, and contributing to

the well-being of local communities can improve
brand image and consumer perception.

19. Innovation and Product Differentiation: Continuous innovation and
product differentiation are essential to maintain
a competitive edge. Companies need to explore
new ideas, technologies, and processes to
enhance their products and services and adapt to
the evolving needs of global consumers.

Each of these points requires specific attention
and strategy, as the challenges and opportunities
presented by globalization are multiple and
complex. Companies must be flexible, resilient,
and ready to innovate to succeed in the
international business landscape.

27. Cultural Adaptation: Cultural adaptation
is essential when entering new markets.
Companies must be aware of cultural, linguistic,
religious, and social diversities and adapt
products, services, and communication
accordingly to avoid misunderstandings and
respect local sensitivities.

28. Localized Research and Development:
Localized research and development can help
create products and services that meet the
specific needs and preferences of local
consumers. This can lead to a more competitive
offering and a stronger brand image at a local
level.

29. Risk Management: Globalization brings a variety of risks, including exchange rate fluctuations, political instability, and differences in regulations. Companies must actively identify and mitigate these risks to protect international operations and maintain financial stability.

30. Transcultural Communication: The ability to communicate effectively across cultural barriers is a key factor for success. Companies must develop transcultural communication skills among employees and with international clients, partners, and suppliers.

31. Competitiveness and Differentiation: In a global market, competitiveness is heightened. Companies must continually seek to differentiate through innovation, quality, service, and sustainability to maintain and gain market share.

32. Digitalization and E-Commerce: Strategic use of digital technology and e-commerce platforms is vital to reach consumers globally. Digitalization can help companies reduce costs, improve efficiency, and provide better services to international customers.

33. Local vs. Global Market Strategies: Companies must balance global strategies with localized approaches, adapting offerings and communication to specific markets while maintaining a cohesive and recognizable brand identity worldwide.

34. Development of International Networks and Relationships: Building and maintaining strong relationships with international partners, customers, and suppliers is crucial. The network of contacts can support business expansion, facilitate access to new markets, and contribute to knowledge and resource sharing.

These are just some of the aspects that companies must consider and carefully manage in the realm of internationalization and globalization. Successfully navigating these areas requires detailed strategic planning, adaptability, and long-term commitment.

35. Positioning Strategies: A proper international positioning strategy is crucial. Companies must analyze how consumers in different regions perceive their brand and adapt positioning based on local culture, values, and consumption behaviors.

36. Tax Regimes and Financial Implications: The diversity of tax regimes among different countries represents a significant challenge. Companies must carefully plan financial structure and business operations to optimize taxes and comply with all local tax laws.

37. Logistics and Supply Chain: Managing logistics and the supply chain at an international level is complex. Supplier selection, inventory management, delivery times, and shipping costs must be optimized to ensure efficiency and customer satisfaction.

38. Multicultural Branding: Branding must be culturally relevant in every market. Companies must understand local symbols, colors, languages, and cultural values to create an appealing and resonating brand with the international audience.

39. Market Analysis and Competitive Intelligence: Gathering and analyzing market and competition data is crucial. Companies must constantly monitor trends, consumer preferences, and competitor strategies to adapt and innovate in real-time.

40. Product Adaptation: Depending on local needs and expectations, it might be necessary to adapt product features, packaging, labels, and instructions for use. This is essential to comply with local regulations and meet consumer expectations.

41. Language Barriers and Communication: Overcoming language barriers is fundamental. Accurate translation of marketing materials, multilingual staff training,

and the use of interpreters can significantly
enhance communication and brand image.

42. Innovation and Local Research:
Investment in local innovation and research is
key. Developing products and services that cater
to the specific needs of different markets can lead
to a competitive advantage and greater
acceptance among local consumers.

43. International Corporate Governance:
Adopting good international corporate
governance practices can strengthen the
company's reputation, enhance stakeholder
relations, and contribute to long-term success in
global markets.

44. Environmental Responsibility:
International companies must consider the
environmental impact of their operations.
Adopting sustainable practices can improve the
brand's image, meet consumer demand, and
comply with local environmental regulations.

**45. Negotiation and Intercompany
Relationships:** The ability to negotiate
effectively and maintain positive relationships
with international partners, distributors, and
customers is essential for successful navigation in
the global business landscape.

In conclusion, internationalization and
globalization are multifaceted processes that
require careful strategy and planning. Companies

must take a holistic approach, considering all aspects of international expansion, from brand positioning to product adaptation, from logistics management to market analysis.

The main challenge lies in balancing brand and offering uniformity with the specifics of local markets. A deep understanding of cultural differences, consumer preferences, and local regulations is essential to establish a strong and lasting presence in new markets. Additionally, considering the tax and financial implications, adopting sustainable and responsible practices, and building strong relationships with suppliers, partners, and customers at the international level is crucial.

Language barriers and communication differences should be addressed with creative and technological solutions, ensuring the brand message is effectively conveyed and the company's values are understood and appreciated. Local innovation and research are also fundamental to developing products and services that meet the specific needs of consumers in different regions.

International corporate governance and environmental responsibility are other crucial pillars of global expansion. Good governance can build stakeholder trust, and sustainability can respond to the growing demand for environmentally responsible products and services, ensuring compliance with local environmental regulations.

Finally, developing negotiation skills and building strong intercompany relationships are essential for success in diverse international markets. The ability to collaborate and negotiate effectively can determine the company's capacity to access new markets, optimize the value chain, and successfully navigate the global business landscape.

In summary, internationalization and globalization are complex and challenging paths that require a well-articulated strategy, in-depth knowledge of local markets, strong ethics, and a continuous ability to adapt and innovate.

18. Crises and Opportunities (COVID-19, Other crises, etc.)

The business world has always been subject to crises and opportunities. Crises, such as the COVID-19 pandemic, have significantly impacted many industries, deeply altering work modes, supply chains, and consumer behaviors. The COVID-19 pandemic, in particular, highlighted the vulnerability of global supply chains and the importance of digitalization. It forced many businesses to adapt their business models, accelerating the transition to e-commerce, remote work, and diversified sourcing. On the other hand, it also created new opportunities, such as increased demand for health products and services, the expansion of the digital technology market, and innovation in sectors like online education and telemedicine. In addition to the pandemic, other crises, such as financial, environmental, or geopolitical ones, can have a significant impact on business. Such crises can generate market uncertainty and volatility, but can also offer opportunities for companies that can adapt and innovate. For example, environmental crises have stimulated the growth of sectors like renewable energies and prompted companies to adopt more sustainable practices. Opportunities also emerge from ongoing technological evolution. Emerging technologies like artificial intelligence, blockchain, and the Internet of Things (IoT) are transforming various sectors, creating new markets and business models. Companies able to leverage these technologies can gain a competitive edge and access new revenue sources. Moreover, demographic and socio-cultural changes can also create crises and opportunities. Population aging, the rise of the global middle class, and increasing attention to social rights and environmental sustainability are influencing the demand for products and services, shaping stakeholder expectations. In conclusion, while crises can bring challenges and uncertainties, they can also act as change and innovation catalysts. Resilient, flexible companies able to anticipate and adapt to changes can not only survive crises but also leverage them to thrive in new market contexts. The key lies in finding a balance between risk management and exploration of new opportunities, always remaining aligned with the company's values and objectives.

Crises and opportunities in the business world are two sides of the same coin. Each crisis presents a unique set of challenges but can also open new doors to unexpected possibilities. Businesses, in their dynamic nature, must be prepared to face the relentless flow of changes and turbulence, taking on many forms.

For instance, consider global trade tensions. These not only influence relationships between countries but also create new market dynamics. Companies may be compelled to reconsider their import-export strategies, seek new suppliers, or diversify their target markets. However, they can also leverage these situations to access new emerging markets or capitalize on opportunities presented by new trade agreements.

Another example is technological innovations. While they radically transform entire sectors, they can also generate inequalities and ethical problems. Therefore, companies must not only continually update themselves on the latest technological trends but also reflect on their social and ethical impact, adapting their practices and strategies accordingly.

The increasing awareness and concern for climate change and sustainability are urging companies to rethink their business models. The transition to a low-carbon economy offers new investment opportunities in renewable energies, sustainable mobility, and green technologies. At the same time, companies must address growing pressures from stakeholders demanding greater transparency and accountability.

Demography and Market Dynamics

Demography is another crucial factor. Population growth in certain world regions and urbanization are leading to new market dynamics but also to challenges such as urban congestion, pollution, and pressure on natural resources. Companies can find opportunities in new market segments and the growing needs of urban consumers, but they must also consider the environmental and social impact of their activities.

Diversification as a Key Strategy

Diversification is a key strategy to navigate through these turbulent waters. Companies diversifying their products, services, and markets are generally more resilient to crises and better positioned to leverage new opportunities. Investing in research and development, staff training, and stakeholder relations are all essential elements for building a resilient and innovative business.

Effective Customer Relationship Management

Effective customer relationship management during crises is vital. Companies must communicate clearly and transparently, demonstrating empathy and support. Customer retention in challenging times can strengthen the company's reputation and contribute to its long-term recovery and growth.

Corporate Culture and Leadership

Corporate culture and leadership also play a crucial role. A culture promoting collaboration, learning, and adaptability can help companies navigate challenges and leverage emerging opportunities. Effective leadership involves guiding with vision and determination, inspiring confidence and motivation during times of uncertainty.

Access to Financing and Resources

Access to financing and resources can make the difference between survival and failure in times of crisis. Prudent financial management, seeking new sources of funding, and diversifying financial risks are all key strategies to ensure the financial sustainability of companies.

These are just some of the aspects that companies need to consider in the context of crises and opportunities. The challenges are numerous and complex, but with the right strategy, vision, and resources, companies can not only overcome crises but also emerge stronger and more resilient.

Reflections on the COVID-19 Pandemic and Business Evolution

Every crisis, such as the one triggered by the COVID-19 pandemic, forces companies to deeply reflect on how to address unprecedented situations. The pandemic accelerated the transition to digital, compelling many companies to rethink how they operate, communicate, and sell their products or services. A new need for agility and flexibility emerged, prompting

businesses to explore new business models, such
as e-commerce, remote work, and technology-
based solutions.

In response to these challenges, many companies
had to reinvent themselves. They adopted
advanced technologies like artificial intelligence,
robotics, and blockchain to improve operational
efficiency, reduce costs, and create new market
opportunities. Digitalization has also led to the
birth of new business models, such as the
subscription economy, allowing companies to
generate recurring income streams and build
closer relationships with customers.

Rapid adaptation was crucial for companies'
survival during the pandemic. They had to
manage the supply chain more efficiently,
optimize resources, cut costs, and find new ways
to interact with customers. The pandemic also
highlighted the importance of resilience and
crisis preparedness, as companies with well-
structured business continuity plans and risk
management strategies were better equipped to
face challenges.

On the other hand, the crisis opened new
opportunities in sectors like digital health, online
education, logistics, and delivery. Companies that
identified and seized these opportunities
expanded their markets and increased their
profits. Product and service diversification,

innovation, and access to new markets became key factors for success in an ever-changing entrepreneurial environment.

Enhanced Focus on Sustainability

Sustainability has become an even more relevant priority during the crisis. Companies are increasingly expected to respond to the growing environmental, social, and governance (ESG) responsibilities from consumers, investors, and society at large. The transition toward more sustainable and responsible business models can not only help companies mitigate risks associated with climate change and social disparities but can also create competitive advantages and growth opportunities.

Essential Role of Partnerships and Collaborations

Partnerships and collaborations have proven essential in overcoming the challenges of the crisis. Companies have sought to establish strategic alliances with complementary partners to expand their market presence, access new skills and resources, and share risks. These collaborations have allowed companies to accelerate innovation, enter new markets, and more effectively meet customer needs.

People Management in Times of Crisis

Finally, people management is another crucial aspect highlighted by the crisis. Companies have had to find new ways to support their employees, promote well-being and productivity, and adapt to new work models. Empathetic leadership, effective communication, and continuous training have become key skills for guiding organizations through uncertain times and building a resilient and inclusive corporate culture.

Conclusion: Managing Crises and Identifying Opportunities

These considerations illustrate the complexity and multidimensionality of crises and opportunities in the business context. While each crisis brings an inevitable share of challenges and uncertainties, it can also act as a catalyst for change and innovation, offering companies the chance to learn, adapt, and grow.

COVID-19 Pandemic: Business Management and Evolution

In conclusion, crisis management and identifying opportunities are essential tasks in today's business landscape, particularly highlighted by the challenges posed by the COVID-19 pandemic. The crisis has revealed the importance of agility, innovation, and adaptability, compelling companies to rethink their business models, adopt new technologies, and diversify products and services. Companies that swiftly adapted, effectively managed the supply chain, optimized resources, and reinvented their customer interactions demonstrated greater resilience. Additionally, the focus on sustainability and corporate social responsibility has become central, with increasing attention to ESG practices and the need to adopt ethical and sustainable business models. This change not only helps mitigate risks associated with climate change and social disparities but also generates competitive advantages, strengthening the corporate image and creating long-term value for stakeholders.

Emerging opportunities in sectors like digital health, online education, and logistics have opened new horizons for proactive businesses. However, identifying and seizing these opportunities requires a deep understanding of the market, strategic vision, and the ability to continuously innovate. Employee training and skill development, along with empathetic and inclusive leadership, are fundamental in building a resilient organization ready to navigate a continuously changing environment.

The importance of partnerships and strategic collaborations has also been reinforced, demonstrating that joining forces with other market players can accelerate innovation, share risks, and access new skills and resources. In an increasingly interconnected and dynamic world, collaboration and co-creation become essential for long-term success.

Finally, the crisis has underscored the need for thorough crisis preparation and management. Companies with well-structured operational continuity plans and effective risk management strategies have been able to navigate uncertainties and position themselves advantageously for the future. Organizational resilience, flexibility, and continuous learning have become key competencies for tackling future challenges and leveraging emerging opportunities.

This comprehensive framework suggests that, while crises may present significant challenges, they also represent moments of learning and growth. With the right strategic approach, companies can not only overcome adversities but also emerge stronger, more resilient, and more sustainable.

19. Product Innovations

Product innovations represent a crucial element for the growth and success of a company in the highly competitive and ever-evolving market. These innovations can take various forms, including significant improvements to existing features, the introduction of new functionalities, or the creation of entirely new products that fulfill an unmet market need.

1. **Technology and Materials**: Adoption of new technologies and materials can lead to more efficient, sustainable, and effective products. For instance, the use of biodegradable materials can reduce environmental impact, while integrating IoT (Internet of Things) technology can make products smarter and more connected.

2. **User-Centered Design**: A user-centered approach to product design can lead to more ergonomic, intuitive, and satisfying solutions for consumers. Research and analysis of user needs and behaviors are fundamental in this process.

3. **Sustainability**: Focus on sustainability has become increasingly important. Innovations that reduce the ecological footprint, utilize renewable resources, and minimize waste can attract conscientious consumers and create a competitive advantage.

4. **Customization**: The ability to personalize products based on individual consumer preferences is a growing trend. Technology has allowed unprecedented levels of customization, from tailor-made products to modular solutions.

5. **Artificial Intelligence and Machine Learning**: Integration of AI and ML can make products smarter, enhancing their performance, customization, and adaptability to user needs.
6. **Omnichannel Solutions**: Designing products that integrate into an omnichannel ecosystem can enhance the customer experience and increase brand loyalty, particularly relevant in sectors like retail and services.
7. **Collaborations and Partnerships**: Collaborating with other companies, universities, or research centers can lead to unique product innovations by combining diverse skills and resources.
8. **Agility and Implementation Speed**: The ability to innovate rapidly and bring new products to market in a short time is a key success factor, especially in fast-evolving sectors like technology and fashion.
9. **Research and Development (R&D)**: Substantial investments in R&D are essential to develop new ideas, test concepts, and prototype innovative solutions. A culture of innovation within the organization is a fundamental driver in this area.
10. **Customer Feedback and Engagement**: Listening to customer feedback and involving them in the product development process can lead to solutions more aligned with their needs

and expectations, thereby increasing satisfaction and loyalty.

11. **Big Data and Analytics**: Data analysis can offer valuable insights into market trends, consumer behaviors, and innovation opportunities, guiding the development of more targeted and competitive products.

In conclusion, product innovation is a complex and multifaceted process requiring a deep understanding of the market, a strong culture of innovation, adoption of new technologies, and a user-centered approach. Companies that succeed in innovating effectively are those that combine strategic vision, creativity, research and development, customer listening, and operational agility, positioning themselves advantageously in today's competitive landscape.

Product innovation certainly doesn't stop at simply conceiving and creating new items; it's rather a vortex of continuous evolution, requiring a deep dive into market dynamics and an incessant quest for excellence. Attention to product line diversification, experimenting with new business models, and constant observation of ever-evolving consumer needs are all strategies that fuel the innovation engine.

Added Value and Differentiation: It's crucial that every new product brings added value to the consumer, offering something unique that sets it apart from the competition. This could mean enhancing quality, offering a unique design, or integrating innovative features that address specific market needs.

Market Validation: Before moving forward with mass production, companies often engage in a market validation phase. This process involves testing the product on a sample of consumers to gather feedback and assess its market acceptance. Validation can help identify potential improvements and optimize the product before its official launch.

Cultural Adaptation: In the era of globalization, cultural adaptation of products is of crucial importance. Companies must be aware of cultural diversities and local preferences, adapting products accordingly to ensure their success in diversified markets.

Product Lifecycle Planning: Product lifecycle management is another critical aspect. From introduction to growth, maturity, and eventually decline, each phase of the product lifecycle requires different marketing, production, and inventory management strategies. Innovation can also involve reinvigorating existing products, extending their life in the market.

Risk Management: Innovation always involves a certain degree of risk. Companies must balance the aspiration for innovation with a thorough assessment of associated risks. This includes evaluating potential negative consequences, managing uncertainty, and preparing for unforeseen scenarios.

Interdisciplinarity and Mixed Skills: Product innovation requires an interdisciplinary approach that combines diverse skills, from research and development to design, marketing to logistics. Creating diversified teams and fostering collaboration across different areas of the company can stimulate creativity and generate innovative solutions.

Flexibility and Scalability: Flexibility and scalability are key elements in the innovation process. Companies must be ready to adapt to market changes and have the ability to quickly scale production in response to demand.

Intellectual Property Protection: Safeguarding innovative ideas through patents, trademarks, and copyrights is essential to maintain a competitive edge and ensure a return on investment.

Ethics and Responsibility: Finally, but no less important, product innovations must be carried out ethically and responsibly, considering social, environmental, and ethical implications. Respect for human rights, environmental protection, and attention to the social impact of

the product are all factors that can influence
consumer acceptance and the company's image.
So, product innovations prove to be a complex
and multifaceted journey, requiring a 360-degree
vision and a holistic approach, considering not
only the technical and commercial aspects but
also the ethical and cultural implications.

Product Innovation Beyond Boundaries

Product innovation transcends the confines of a
single sector, embracing emerging technologies
and cross-functional applications. Each product
innovation can be considered a small revolution
that shifts the existing paradigm and opens new
possibilities and horizons.

Sustainable Development: An area gaining
momentum in product innovation is sustainable
development. Companies are increasingly
exploring ways to produce goods more
ecologically, using recyclable or biodegradable
materials, and reducing the use of non-renewable
resources. The goal is to reduce the ecological
footprint and create products that harmonize
with the environment and society.

Technological Integration: Incorporating
new technologies into products is another key
element of innovation. Whether it's artificial
intelligence, the Internet of Things, or
augmented and virtual reality, integrating
advanced technologies can enhance product

functionalities and offer unique experiences to users.

Personalization and Customization: The trend toward personalization and customization is gaining ground. Consumers desire products that adapt to their individual needs and preferences. The ability to offer tailored products or customization options can be a strong market differentiator.

Collaborations and Partnerships: Collaborations between companies and establishing partnerships can lead to synergistic product innovations. By pooling skills and resources, companies can develop products beyond what they could have achieved individually. Collaborations can occur not only with other companies but also with universities, research centers, and innovative startups.

Big Data Analysis: Big data analysis plays a crucial role in identifying new product innovation opportunities. Through the analysis of large data sets, companies can identify emerging trends, better understand consumer needs, and forecast future market developments.

Customer Feedback and Engagement: Customer involvement in the innovation process is fundamental. Collecting feedback, listening to consumer needs and opinions can offer valuable insights for new product development.

Companies are increasingly adopting co-creative approaches, involving customers in the ideation and product development phase.

Agility and Iteration: Adopting an agile and iterative approach in product development can accelerate the innovation process. Experimenting, testing, prototyping, receiving feedback, and making continuous improvements allows the product to adapt to the evolving market needs and reduces the risk of failure.

Competition and Benchmarking: Finally, observing the competition and benchmarking can offer valuable insights for product innovation. Studying competitors' products, identifying their strengths and weaknesses, and aiming to surpass them can be a powerful driver for innovation.

This way, product innovation appears as a mosaic of factors and influences that, if well orchestrated, can lead to market success and bolster the company's competitive position. In the context of product innovation, it's crucial to consider the importance of intellectual property, design thinking, and the significance of a multidisciplinary approach.

Intellectual Property: The protection of intellectual property is crucial to safeguard innovations. Patents, trademarks, and copyrights are essential tools to protect ideas and ensure that the company can derive maximum benefits from its innovations. Effective management of intellectual property can also facilitate collaboration and licensing, allowing companies to expand the scope of their innovations.

Design Thinking: Design thinking is an approach that centers around human needs and focuses the product development process on solving real user problems. Through empathy, problem definition, ideation, prototyping, and testing, design thinking allows the development of innovative solutions that truly address people's needs.

Multidisciplinary Approach: Product innovation significantly benefits from a multidisciplinary approach. Involving experts from different disciplines, from engineers to designers, from marketers to data scientists, can lead to more comprehensive and well-thought-out solutions. The intersection of diverse areas of knowledge is often the fertile ground for the birth of the most innovative ideas.

Research and Development: Investing in research and development is another fundamental pillar of product innovation. R&D enables the exploration of new technologies, materials, and methodologies, laying the groundwork for cutting-edge product development. Leading companies in innovation tend to allocate a significant percentage of their resources to R&D.

Market Trends and Competitive Analysis: Keeping up with market trends and conducting regular competitive analyses are essential practices to identify innovation opportunities. Understanding market dynamics and anticipating changes in consumer demand can give companies a competitive edge and guide the development of new products.

Product Life Cycle: Effectively managing the product life cycle is essential. From ideation to production, from marketing to market withdrawal, each phase of the life cycle requires careful management to maximize product success. Innovation can occur at every stage of the life cycle, improving the efficiency, quality, and relevance of the product in the market.

Adoption of Emerging Technologies: Exploring and adopting emerging technologies can open new possibilities for innovation. Blockchain, 3D printing, advanced robotics, and nanotechnology are just a few of the technologies revolutionizing various sectors and offering new opportunities for innovative product development.

Innovation Ecosystem: Finally, creating and participating in an innovation ecosystem, which includes incubators, accelerators, universities, research centers, and other innovative companies, can stimulate idea generation and facilitate access to essential resources and expertise for product innovation.

In this landscape, product innovation becomes a complex and multifaceted journey, rich in challenges and opportunities, where creativity, knowledge, collaboration, and strategic vision are key ingredients for success.

Product innovation goes beyond mere creation; it encompasses a range of factors and facets that play crucial roles in a product's development and success in the market. Each element, from prototyping to customer feedback analysis, contributes to forming a complete picture of product innovation.

Adaptability and Flexibility: In a market of continuous change and development, the ability to adapt rapidly to new trends and demands is vital. Flexibility in rethinking and adapting products enables companies to remain competitive and relevant, accommodating shifts in consumer tastes and preferences.

Environmental Sustainability: In an era of growing environmental awareness, incorporating sustainable practices in design and production is crucial. Sustainability isn't just ethically responsible but can also offer a competitive advantage, attracting conscious consumers and creating a positive brand image.

Customer Collaboration: Interaction and collaboration with customers during the product development process can lead to remarkable outcomes. Customer insights offer a valuable perspective and help shape a product that truly meets their needs and expectations.

Artificial Intelligence and Big Data: The use of artificial intelligence and big data can provide invaluable insights into consumer behavior, guiding companies in developing tailored products. These technologies enable the analysis of vast amounts of data to identify patterns and trends that inform strategic decisions and enhance innovation effectiveness.

Testing and Validation: A thorough testing and validation phase is essential to ensure the product is market-ready. This phase helps identify and resolve any issues, ensuring the final product meets quality standards and consumer expectations.

Crowdfunding and Financing Platforms: Crowdfunding has become an increasingly popular means to fund product innovation. Platforms like Kickstarter and Indiegogo allow companies to present their ideas to a global audience, securing funding and market validation before the actual product launch.

Return on Investment Analysis: Carefully assessing the return on investment (ROI) is crucial for every product innovation. In-depth ROI analysis helps companies understand the value generated by innovation and effectively manage resources.

Training and Skill Development: Continual training and development of product development teams are crucial. Promoting a learning environment and enhancing skills can improve creativity and productivity, contributing to product innovation success.

Each of these elements contributes to shaping the complex landscape of product innovation, emphasizing the importance of a holistic and well-considered approach to navigate successfully in this domain.

In conclusion, product innovation represents a complex and multifaceted set of activities, processes, and strategies that go well beyond the mere creation of a new item. It's a dynamic and evolving process that requires a holistic approach and forward-thinking to ensure success in the current and future market.

Multidisciplinary Integration: A key factor in product innovation is multidisciplinary integration involving various areas like design, engineering, marketing, and sales. This synergy among different disciplines ensures that every aspect of the product is optimized and aligned with the overall company objectives.

Agility and Execution Speed: Organizational agility and swiftness in implementation are vital to keeping up with competition and promptly responding to market needs. Companies need to accelerate product development cycles while maintaining high standards of quality and compliance.

Research and Development (R&D): Investments in research and development are essential to fuel innovation and maintain a competitive edge. R&D enables companies to explore new technologies, materials, and methodologies, laying the foundation for groundbreaking product development.

Customer Experience: Customer experience should be at the heart of the innovation process. Understanding customer expectations, needs, and desires is crucial to develop products that are truly appealing and provide added value.

Intellectual Property: Management and protection of intellectual property are fundamental to safeguarding the company's innovations. Patents, trademarks, and copyrights are essential tools to protect innovation investments and prevent imitation by competitors.

Measurement and Success Evaluation: Lastly, it's imperative to establish clear metrics and performance indicators to measure and evaluate the success of product innovation. This includes not only sales and profit assessments but also analysis of brand impact, market share, and customer satisfaction.

In summary, product innovation is an intricate and multifaceted journey that demands a well-articulated strategy, constant commitment, and proactive vision. Companies that successfully navigate this path are those that adopt an integrated approach, value multidisciplinary collaboration, and are always ready to adapt to changes while maintaining a strong commitment to quality, sustainability, and customer satisfaction.

20. Packaging and Labeling

Packaging and labeling are essential aspects in product management and marketing. It's not just about protecting and preserving the product but also effectively communicating the brand and information to consumers, influencing the perception of value and purchasing decisions.

Primary Functions: The primary functions of packaging include product protection during transportation and distribution, preservation of properties and product functionality, and facilitating consumer use. Labeling, on the other hand, provides essential product information such as ingredients, usage instructions, warnings, and regulatory information.

Brand Communication: Packaging design is a powerful tool for brand communication. Colors, shapes, materials, and graphics play a crucial role in product positioning and creating an emotional connection with consumers. Well-designed packaging can increase product visibility on shelves and differentiate it from competitors.

Environmental Sustainability: The growing environmental awareness has led to renewed interest in sustainable packaging. Recyclable, biodegradable, and low-impact environmental materials are increasingly sought after by conscientious consumers. Companies are adopting eco-friendly packaging solutions to meet demand and reduce ecological impact.

Regulations and Standards: Packaging and labeling regulations are strict and vary by country and product type. Clear, complete, and compliant labels are essential to avoid legal sanctions and ensure consumer safety and information.

Technology and Innovation: Technological innovation has introduced new packaging solutions like augmented reality, QR codes, and smart packaging that can interact with consumers and provide additional information and interactive experiences.

Market Testing and Consumer Feedback: Conducting market tests and gathering consumer feedback is crucial to optimize packaging design and ensure it meets the expectations and needs of the target audience. This process can lead to improvements and adaptations that increase product acceptance in the market.

Costs and Logistic Efficiency: Finally, cost management and logistical efficiency are crucial aspects in packaging design. The choice of materials, packaging shape, and size influences not only production costs but also ease of transport, preservation, and product display. Continuing to explore this broad topic reveals additional facets and considerations that reflect the complexity and importance of the role of packaging and labeling in the contemporary business landscape.

In addition to the functions and aspects already outlined, packaging and labeling also intersect with various areas of interest in the business context, impacting factors such as brand perception, consumer experience, and legal compliance.

Value Addition and Differentiation: A significant aspect of packaging is its ability to add value to the product. Through creativity and design, packaging can create a unique experience for the consumer, promoting differentiation in the market. The perception of uniqueness and quality can incentivize consumer preference and justify a premium price.

Multisensory Packaging: Multisensory experience is an emerging concept in packaging design. Combining textures, colors, sounds, and scents can stimulate the consumer's senses, creating a lasting memory and influencing product perception. The ongoing research for innovative materials and advanced printing techniques contributes to developing packaging that engages consumers at multiple sensory levels.

Traceability and Security: Product traceability is a key element, especially in sectors like food and pharmaceuticals. Integrating technologies like RFID and blockchain into packaging allows tracking product origin, distribution, and history, ensuring authenticity and security. These technological solutions help prevent counterfeiting and enhance consumer confidence.

Customization and Limited Editions: Customization of packaging is a growing trend, catering to consumers' desire for unique and distinctive products. Launching limited editions, celebratory packaging, and personalized designs creates a sense of exclusivity, fueling market interest and curiosity. This strategy can be particularly effective in launching new products or boosting sales on special occasions.

Consumer Awareness and Information: Packaging and labeling are effective tools to raise consumer awareness about issues like environmental sustainability, health, and well-being. Transparency and clarity in the information provided can educate the consumer and influence conscious choices. The use of symbols, certifications, and educational messages contributes to creating a dialogue between the brand and the consumer, building a relationship based on trust and shared values.

Inclusive Design and Accessibility: Another significant consideration in packaging design is inclusivity and accessibility. Designing packaging that is easy to open, use, and read is essential to ensure accessibility for all consumers, including the elderly and people with disabilities. Paying attention to the needs of different consumer groups can improve the brand's reputation and expand the target market.

Market Trend Response: Finally, it is crucial for packaging and labeling to be able to adapt and respond to evolving market trends. Market analysis and monitoring emerging trends allow anticipating changes in consumer behavior and developing innovative packaging solutions aligned with market expectations.

The multifunctionality of packaging and labeling, their intersection with various areas of business management, and their capacity to influence consumer perception and behavior make them a strategic element in defining the success of a product in the contemporary market.

Sustainability and Eco-friendly Materials: In an era of growing environmental awareness, sustainable packaging has become imperative. Companies are exploring the use of biodegradable, recyclable, and renewable materials, aiming to reduce environmental impact. Using eco-friendly inks, less polluting adhesives, and low-energy consumption production processes contributes to creating a greener packaging system.

Innovation and Technology: The packaging sector is continuously evolving, thanks to the introduction of new technologies and innovative processes. For instance, augmented reality can be incorporated into packaging to offer an interactive experience to consumers, providing additional content, promotions, or information. 3D printing is also revolutionizing packaging production, allowing greater customization and flexibility in design.

Regulatory Compliance: It is essential for packaging and labels to comply with local and international regulations. Compliance with laws on food safety, product chemical labeling, and material use restrictions is crucial to avoid legal sanctions and damage to the company's reputation. Understanding and continuous updating of legislation are, therefore, essential aspects.

Brand Communication: Packaging is one of the most direct communication tools between the brand and the consumer. It reflects the brand's personality, values, and mission. Well-designed packaging can tell a story, convey emotions, and create an emotional connection with the consumer, influencing brand loyalty and purchase decisions.

Adaptability and Versatility: The adaptability of packaging is crucial in a rapidly evolving market. Companies must be able to quickly adapt packaging to new formats, sizes, and distribution channels. Versatility in design allows prompt response to changes in demand, customization needs, and distribution requirements.

Supply Chain Efficiency: The design of packaging also influences supply chain efficiency. Designing packaging that optimizes space in transportation, is damage-resistant, and facilitates handling and storage can reduce logistics costs and minimize environmental impact.

Research and Development: Investing in research and development is vital to keeping pace with packaging innovation. Exploring new materials, testing new design solutions, and developing new production processes can lead to groundbreaking discoveries and provide a sustainable competitive advantage.

Consumer Feedback: Listening to consumer feedback is essential to develop packaging that meets their needs and expectations. Social media, online reviews, and surveys are valuable tools to gather opinions and suggestions that can guide design decisions and improve the product's perception.

These elements, together with those already mentioned, underline the complexity and importance of packaging and labeling in today's business landscape, highlighting how every detail can have a significant impact on product performance and the consumer relationship.

Emerging Trends and Challenges in Packaging and Labeling: In the modern and dynamic world of packaging and labeling, there are always new emerging trends and challenges. The growing consumer demand for transparency and traceability, for instance, is driving companies to implement advanced labeling and coding systems. QR and RFID technologies are tools that allow consumers to access detailed product information, including its origin and sustainability, contributing to building trust and loyalty.
Concurrently, the emergence of new consumer models and distribution channels such as e-commerce presents unique challenges in terms of packaging. The need for sturdy packaging that protects the product during transportation but is easy to open for the consumer is a delicate balance to achieve. Furthermore, packaging should consider the unboxing experience, increasingly valued by online consumers.
Customization: Customization is another key trend in the packaging industry. The ability to create unique and personalized packaging can

help companies differentiate themselves from the competition and build a closer relationship with consumers. Digital printing technologies are making customization more accessible and cost-effective, even for small print runs.

Color Psychology in Packaging: It is also important not to underestimate the importance of color psychology in packaging. Colors can influence consumers' emotions and purchasing decisions. A profound understanding of color psychology and how consumers react to different colors can help create packaging that captures attention and effectively communicates the brand's message.

Smart and Connected Packaging: Smart and connected packaging represents the future of the sector. The integration of sensors, chips, and other technologies in packaging will allow monitoring product conditions, tracking its location, and communicating real-time information. This technological evolution could revolutionize sectors such as food and pharmaceuticals, where product preservation is crucial.

Collaboration and Creativity: Lastly, collaboration with designers, artists, and influencers can open new creative possibilities and offer unique perspectives in packaging design. These partnerships can result in artistic and innovative packaging that captures consumers' imagination and elevates the product into a work of art.

In summary, the world of packaging and labeling is a constantly evolving field, full of opportunities and challenges, where innovation, creativity, and sustainability play an increasingly central role. Companies that successfully navigate this complex landscape will have the opportunity to build lasting relationships with consumers and gain a competitive advantage in the market.

Sustainability in Packaging and Labeling: Another key element in the field of packaging and labeling is sustainability. More and more consumers are showing interest and concern for the environment, leading companies to explore eco-friendly packaging options. Biodegradable, recyclable, and reusable materials are increasingly sought after, and packaging design is evolving to reduce the use of plastic and other environmentally harmful materials. Eco-friendly certifications can also offer added value and contribute to building a positive brand reputation.

Evolving Regulations in Packaging and Labeling: The continually evolving regulation is also a crucial consideration in the field of packaging and labeling. Companies must keep up with local, national, and international laws and regulations, which may concern product information labeling, material safety, and disposal practices. Non-compliance can lead to penalties, product recalls, and damage to the brand's reputation.

Technological Innovations and Design: Technological innovation in printing and packaging production is opening up new possibilities. For example, 3D printing can allow the creation of customized and highly personalized packaging. New printing techniques can also enhance image quality and detail, making labels more attractive and informative.

Augmented Reality Integration: The integration of augmented reality (AR) into packaging is another innovation gaining ground. Through smartphone apps, consumers can interact with packaging, accessing additional multimedia content, in-depth product information, and interactive experiences. This not only enriches the consumer experience but also offers new marketing and engagement opportunities for companies.

Inclusive Design: Inclusive design is another crucial consideration. Creating packaging and labels accessible to people with disabilities, such as those with visual or motor impairments, is essential for inclusivity and can also open up new market segments. The use of legible fonts, contrasting colors, and tactile features can enhance packaging accessibility.

Data-Driven Design and AI: Companies are also exploring the use of artificial intelligence (AI) and data analytics to optimize packaging design. By analyzing consumer behavior, preferences, and market trends, companies can make more informed decisions about packaging design, materials, and functionality, maximizing impact and effectiveness.

Supply Chain Management: Furthermore, the management of the packaging supply chain is crucial. Companies must closely collaborate with material suppliers, manufacturers, and distributors to ensure quality, compliance, and cost efficiency. Adopting sustainable sourcing practices can reduce environmental impact and enhance the brand's image.

Consumer Education: Finally, consumer training and education play a fundamental role. Educating consumers about proper use, reuse, and recycling of packaging can help reduce waste and environmental impact, strengthening the relationship between consumers and brands. Transparency and proactive communication are essential in this educational process.

In summary, the packaging and labeling sector is fertile ground for innovation, creativity, and sustainability. Emerging trends and technologies offer numerous opportunities for companies to differentiate, create value, and meet growing consumer expectations and environmental challenges.

Multisensory Marketing in Packaging: In the context of packaging and labeling, sensory marketing plays a fundamental role. Companies are experimenting with materials, textures, and printing techniques that stimulate the senses, creating a multisensory experience that can strengthen brand identity and consumer engagement. Packaging can evoke tactile, olfactory, and even auditory sensations, contributing to memorability and differentiation in the market.

Product Safety and Traceability:
Simultaneously, product safety is another critical aspect. Packaging must protect the content from damage, contamination, and alterations, ensuring the safety and integrity of the product until it reaches the final consumer. Sturdy materials, security seals, and anti-fraud technologies are increasingly implemented to prevent risks and ensure consumer trust.

Product Traceability and Transparency:
Product traceability and transparency have become priorities for many consumers. Traceability technologies like QR codes and blockchain allow tracking the origin, production,

and distribution of products. This enhances transparency, enabling consumers to access detailed information about the provenance and sustainability of the products they purchase.

Practicality and Usability: The issue of the practicality and usability of packaging is also fundamental. In an increasingly fast-paced and interconnected world, consumers seek packaging solutions that are easy to open, use, and transport. Packaging design must therefore consider the need for practicality and convenience, especially in sectors like food and healthcare, where ease of use can significantly influence consumer choice.

Cultural and Demographic Considerations: Cultural and demographic considerations also influence perceptions and expectations regarding packaging and labeling. Companies operating on a global scale must be able to adapt the design, messages, and label information to diverse cultures and local regulations, ensuring brand consistency and respect for cultural differences.

Psychology of Colors: The psychology of colors is another element not to be underestimated in packaging design. Each color evokes different emotions and reactions, and color choices can influence brand perception, product visibility on shelves, and consumer purchasing decisions. Companies invest in research and analysis to identify the most effective colors in relation to their target markets and branding goals.

Evolution of Consumer Habits: Moreover, the evolution of consumption habits, such as the increase in online shopping, is influencing the design and functionality of packaging. E-commerce packaging must ensure greater protection during transport while also offering a memorable unboxing experience. Customizing packaging with unique messages and designs can contribute to creating an emotional connection with the consumer and strengthening brand loyalty.

Corporate Social Responsibility (CSR): With the growing importance of corporate social responsibility, companies are increasingly called upon to demonstrate their commitment to society and the environment through their packaging choices. Communicating sustainable initiatives, social responsibility projects, and partnerships with environmental organizations can be conveyed through packaging and labels, contributing to building a positive and responsible brand image.

Brand Communication and Promotion: Lastly, packaging and labeling are key tools for brand communication and promotion. Through design, messages, colors, and images, packaging conveys the values and personality of the brand, helping create a distinctive positioning in the market and establishing a dialogue with consumers. Consistency between packaging, brand identity, and communication strategy is fundamental for long-term success in today's competitive market.

Concluding Thoughts

In conclusion, packaging and labeling are not merely protective covers or informational tools; they play a multidimensional role in a product's value and a brand's success. They serve not only to preserve and protect the product but also to communicate, attract, and build relationships with consumers. The functions of packaging and labeling are interconnected, influencing each other, determining the perceived value and the consumer's purchasing experience.

Sustainability

Sustainability has become a fundamental pillar of packaging strategy. Companies are called upon to meet growing environmental demands through innovation and reducing ecological impact, adopting recyclable materials, low-energy production processes, and waste reduction solutions. Attention to sustainability is not only an ethical obligation but also an opportunity for differentiation and brand enhancement in the market.

Personalization and Technology

Personalization and technology are transforming how packaging and labels interact with consumers. The integration of digital elements, augmented reality, and advanced traceability offers new possibilities for engagement, loyalty, and brand enhancement. These innovations allow the creation of unique and memorable experiences that go beyond simple commercial transactions and contribute to building lasting relationships with consumers.

Practicality, Usability, and Safety

The importance of practicality, usability, and safety cannot be underestimated. Packaging must ensure product protection as well as ease of use and transport. These aspects directly influence consumer satisfaction and can determine the success or failure of a product in the market.

Cultural and Demographic Sensitivity

Sensitivity to cultural and demographic differences is fundamental for a global brand. The ability to adapt packaging and labels to local regulations and consumer expectations is a strategic competence that can open new markets and growth opportunities.

Consistency and Alignment

Finally, consistency and alignment between packaging, brand identity, and communication strategy are essential to build a strong and distinctive brand. Packaging is a key touchpoint in the consumer's purchasing journey and must reflect the values, mission, and vision of the brand, contributing to strengthening the market position and consumer loyalty.

In conclusion, packaging and labeling are strategic elements that integrate various aspects of marketing, production, logistics, and corporate social responsibility. The evolution of technologies, consumer habits, and environmental challenges is shaping the future of packaging, making it increasingly central to creating value and the success of companies in the global market.

22. Future Trends and Perspectives

Future trends in the field of business and marketing are characterized by rapid technological development, growing consumer expectations, and increased attention to the social and environmental impact of companies. Below are some of the most relevant trends and perspectives for the future:

1. **Sustainability and Social Responsibility:** Sustainability will continue to be a priority, with increasing interest in the circular economy. Companies must adopt ecologically sustainable and ethically responsible practices to remain competitive and meet the growing expectations of consumers and global regulations.

2. **Artificial Intelligence and Machine Learning:** AI and machine learning will have a significant impact on data analysis, marketing personalization, automation of business processes, and the creation of new business models. These technologies will enable companies to be more efficient, innovative, and responsive to market changes.

3. **E-commerce and Mobile Commerce:** E-commerce and m-commerce will continue to grow, driven by the evolution of digital technologies, increased connectivity, and changes in consumer buying habits. Online presence and the ability to offer seamless shopping experiences will become increasingly crucial.

4. **Customer Experience and Personalization:** Customer experience and personalization will be at the center of marketing strategies. Companies must focus on a customer-

centric approach, using data and technologies to better understand consumer needs and offer personalized products, services, and content.

5. **Blockchain and Decentralized Technologies:** Blockchain and other decentralized technologies could revolutionize sectors such as finance, logistics, and supply chain, offering more secure, transparent, and efficient solutions. These technologies have the potential to create new business and governance models.

6. **Remote Working and New Work Dynamics:** Remote working and work flexibility will become more common, requiring companies to adopt new tools, policies, and organizational cultures. These new dynamics will impact talent attraction and retention, productivity, and employee well-being.

7. **Health and Wellness:** The growing focus on health and wellness will influence consumer behavior and product offerings. Companies must consider the impact of their products and services on the physical and mental health of consumers and communities.

8. **Globalization and Localization:** The tension between globalization and localization will continue to characterize the international landscape. Companies must balance global strategies with local needs, adapting products,

services, and communication to different markets and cultures.

9. **Crises and Emergencies:** Preparedness for crises and business resilience will be increasingly important, considering the rise of global challenges such as pandemics, climate change, and geopolitical conflicts. Companies must develop emergency plans, diversify risks, and invest in long-term sustainability.

10. **Innovation and Research & Development:** Innovation will continue to be a key driver of competitiveness. Companies must invest in research and development, explore new ideas and technologies, and create products and services that meet emerging market needs.

In summary, future trends in the business world outline an ever-evolving landscape where technology, sustainability, personalization, and resilience will be central themes. Companies must be flexible, innovative, and responsible to navigate successfully in this complex and dynamic scenario.

The rapid evolution of the business landscape continues to reveal new horizons and challenges, introducing different concepts and unexpected opportunities. Further exploration

unveils some other significant trends that might influence the future of business:

21.**Platform Economy:** The platform economy is strengthening, with companies acting as digital intermediaries, connecting different users and creating value through this mediation. Platforms like Uber, Airbnb, and Amazon are examples of this model that will continue to proliferate in diverse sectors.

22. **Big Data and Advanced Analytics:** The increasing accumulation of data offers unprecedented opportunities for predictive and prescriptive analysis, improving decision-making and enabling greater customer offer customization.

23. **Cybersecurity and Privacy:** In the digital era, data protection and privacy become increasingly critical. Companies will need to invest in advanced cybersecurity solutions and ensure compliance with data protection regulations to maintain customer trust and prevent breaches.

24. **Digital Health:** Technology integration in the healthcare sector is revolutionizing patient care, diagnosis, and disease management. The use of apps, wearables, and telemedicine demonstrates how technology can improve access and healthcare quality.

25.   **Online Education and Continuous Learning:** Online learning and continuous education are essential to keep skills updated in an ever-evolving job market. Online education platforms like Coursera and Udemy are gaining popularity, and companies are investing in employee training and development.

26.   **Subscription Economy:** The adoption of subscription-based business models is growing in various sectors, from media to video streaming and software. This model allows for recurring revenue streams and the creation of long-term customer relationships.

27.   **Collaboration and Strategic Partnerships:** Collaboration between companies, startups, universities, and research institutes can accelerate innovation and access to new markets. Strategic partnerships become essential for sharing resources, skills, and risks.

28.   **Inclusion and Diversity:** Inclusion and diversity are increasingly important for corporate culture. Companies recognize the value of diversity of thought and are adopting practices to promote equality and inclusion in the workplace.

29.   **AgriTech and Sustainable Development:** Innovation in the agricultural sector is essential to address challenges such as food security and climate change. Technology can

improve productivity, reduce waste, and promote sustainable agricultural practices.

30. **Urbanization and Smart Cities:** Urbanization continues to accelerate, and smart cities use technology to improve quality of life, optimize resource use, and manage growth sustainably.

31. These trends outline a future scenario of continuous transformation, where the ability to adapt, innovate, and maintain social and ethical responsibility will determine success in the global market. Every company, regardless of the sector, will need to navigate this complex environment, considering the impact of these trends on their business model and operational strategy.

32. Certainly, I will continue to delve into the theme of future trends and prospects in the business world, exploring further dynamics and emerging developments:

33. **Artificial Intelligence and Automation:** AI and automation continue to mature, offering increasingly advanced tools for companies to optimize processes, reduce costs, and improve customer experience. This technological evolution requires reflection on potential ethical and social impacts, such as job losses and privacy issues.

34. **Blockchain and DLT Technologies:** Distributed ledger technologies like blockchain

are finding applications in various sectors beyond cryptocurrencies, including finance, healthcare, supply chain, and digital rights management. These technologies promise greater transaction transparency, security, and traceability.

35. **Renewable Energy and Energy Transition:** Growing concerns about climate change and sustainability are driving a radical change in the energy sector. Investment in renewable energy sources and energy storage technologies is increasing, and the electrification of transport is gaining ground.

36. **Personalization and Customization:** Consumer expectations for personalized products and services are fueling innovation in various sectors. Technology enables greater customization in areas like clothing, food, and education, enhancing customer satisfaction.

37. **Biotech and Genomics:** Advances in life sciences, biotechnology, and genomics are revolutionizing medicine, agriculture, and synthetic biology. The ability to modify DNA and develop genetic therapies opens new ethical and therapeutic frontiers.

38. Sustainable Development and Circular Economy: The need for a more sustainable economic model is driving the adoption of circular economy practices. Waste reduction, recycling, and reusing are becoming imperative for companies aiming to minimize their environmental impact and meet consumer expectations.

39. Food Safety and Sustainable Agriculture: The increasing demand for food and the need for sustainable agricultural practices are driving innovation in the agricultural sector. Precision farming, urban agriculture, and alternative proteins are just some emerging solutions.

40. Sustainable and Experiential Tourism: The tourism sector is evolving towards more sustainable and experience-oriented models. Experiential tourism, ecotourism, and cultural tourism are gaining popularity as destinations and tourism businesses work to reduce their environmental impact.

41. Future Mobility and Autonomous Vehicles: Urban mobility is undergoing radical transformation with the development of autonomous vehicles, drones, hyperloop, and other innovative transportation solutions. These changes pose new challenges in terms of infrastructure, regulations, and safety.

42. Aging Population and Healthcare: Increased life expectancy and the global aging population create new challenges and opportunities in the healthcare sector.

Telemedicine, preventive medicine, and digital health are key strategies to address these challenges.

These developments highlight the importance for businesses to stay ahead, anticipating trends and proactively adapting to market changes and consumer needs. The ability to innovate and responsibly integrate new technologies will be crucial for long-term success.

In conclusion, carefully examining future trends and prospects is essential for any business entity aspiring to thrive in an ever-changing and highly competitive market environment. Analyzing emerging trends offers the opportunity to anticipate market transformations, adapt business strategies, and stay ahead of the competition.

Among the most significant trends, Artificial Intelligence, Blockchain, energy transition, and advancements in biotechnology represent changing factors that can redefine entire industrial sectors, creating new market opportunities but also challenges in terms of adaptability and regulatory compliance. It is essential for companies to understand how these trends will impact not only their industry but also society as a whole, as corporate social responsibility is increasingly at the center of consumer and stakeholder expectations.

Furthermore, the increasing focus on sustainability and sustainable development implies a profound rethinking of current business practices. Adopting a circular economy model, implementing sustainable agricultural and tourism practices, as well as innovating in the field of mobility, are essential to reduce environmental impact and meet the needs of an increasingly aware and demanding society.

The growing demand for personalization and the transformation of consumption models require greater flexibility and the ability to offer tailor-made products and services while maintaining high quality and ethical standards. This is particularly relevant in sectors like healthcare, where the aging population and growing healthcare expectations are shaping new business paradigms and opportunities.

In summary, navigating through these future trends and perspectives requires a strategic vision, a deep understanding of the socio-economic and technological context, and the willingness to innovate and adapt continually. Businesses that manage to anticipate and embrace these changes will be better positioned to create long-term value, build strong relationships with customers and stakeholders, and contribute significantly to building a sustainable and inclusive future.

23. Competition and Differentiation

Competition and differentiation are fundamental concepts in the business world, representing key elements for a company's success in a saturated and competitive market.
Competition is the interaction between companies operating in the same sector, competing for market share, customers, and resources. It can be direct, with companies offering similar products or services, or indirect, competing to satisfy the same need with different solutions. In a highly competitive market environment, companies must continuously adapt, innovate, and improve their offerings to maintain and grow their market position.
Differentiation, on the other hand, is the strategy by which a company seeks to distinguish itself from the competition by offering unique, higher quality, or personalized products or services, or through branding, marketing, and customer service. An effective differentiation strategy can allow a company to establish a competitive advantage, justify premium prices, and create brand loyalty among consumers.
In the current context, characterized by rapid technological changes and the globalization of markets, competition has intensified and taken

new forms. E-commerce, digital platforms, and Artificial Intelligence have broken entry barriers, enabling new players to emerge and challenge traditional companies. Moreover, access to detailed consumer information has made marketing and advertising more targeted and personalized, increasing competitive pressure. To address these challenges, companies must proactively seek new differentiation opportunities. Product innovation, the adoption of emerging technologies, environmental and social sustainability, and customer experience have become key factors for setting themselves apart from the competition. Attention to corporate social responsibility and the adoption of ethical practices can also contribute to building a positive brand image and establishing trust relationships with customers and stakeholders.

In conclusion, the ability to understand the dynamics of competition and implement effective differentiation strategies is essential for the survival and long-term success of companies in today's market. Maintaining an innovative approach, being attentive to consumer needs and values, and building strong relationships are all elements that can contribute to solidifying a company's position in a competitive and ever-evolving environment.

In the context of competition and differentiation, the perception of value by the customer plays a central role. To remain competitive, companies must deeply understand the needs, expectations, and preferences of their target markets and structure their offerings to maximize perceived value. This may include not only the quality and characteristics of the product or service but also aspects such as customer service, brand reputation, and social responsibility. Additionally, in an era characterized by simplified access to information and increased consumer awareness, companies must be transparent and authentic in their communications and actions. Any attempt to manipulate or deceive consumers can be quickly uncovered and spread, damaging the company's reputation and customer trust.

Another crucial aspect of differentiation is personalization. With the advent of digital technologies and big data, companies have the ability to collect and analyze vast amounts of consumer data, enabling them to personalize offerings and communications more precisely. This personalization can help create a closer bond between the company and the customer, increasing loyalty and propensity to spend.

Beyond Personalization: Continual Innovation

Continuous innovation is another cornerstone of differentiation. In saturated and rapidly changing markets, companies that manage to innovate constantly, both in terms of products and processes, have a greater chance to distinguish themselves from the competition and remain relevant to consumers' eyes. Innovation can relate not only to technological aspects but also to business models, value chains, and strategic partnerships.

Globalization and Internationalization

In an increasingly globalized landscape, internationalization can also be seen as a form of differentiation. Companies expanding their presence in different markets can benefit from economies of scale, access to new customer segments, and risk diversification. However, internationalization also presents significant challenges, such as the need to adapt to diverse cultures, regulations, and market dynamics.

Sustainability as a Competitive Factor

Finally, environmental and social sustainability have become increasingly important elements of differentiation. Modern consumers are increasingly attentive to the impact that products and companies have on the planet and society, and many companies are responding to this trend by integrating sustainable practices into every aspect of their operations. Sustainability is no longer just an ethical issue but has become a genuine competitive factor.

Market Dynamics and Technological Evolution

Competition and differentiation in the business world are also strongly influenced by digital market dynamics and technological evolution. In an era where online presence is crucial, digital marketing strategies and online reputation management have become central in distinguishing from the competition. Companies are significantly investing in SEO, quality content, social media marketing, and other digital tactics to attract and retain customers.

Customer Experience and Value Perception

Moreover, customer experience has become a crucial battleground for companies. Providing an excellent customer experience, both online and offline, can be a determining factor in acquiring and retaining customer loyalty. This includes the user-friendliness of websites and apps, customer service, personalization, and the ability to swiftly resolve any issues. Companies that fail to meet customer expectations regarding experience risk losing ground to competitors who do so.

Value Chain Management and Intellectual Property

Value chain management is another aspect that can create differentiation. Companies that optimize and innovate their value chains can reduce costs, improve efficiency, and consequently offer products and services at more competitive prices or with higher profit margins. Sustainable sourcing, lean production, and efficient resource utilization are factors that can contribute to creating a competitive advantage. Concurrently, intellectual property is a crucial element of differentiation. Companies invest significant resources in research and development to create patentable products, services, and technologies that can offer unique advantages not easily replicable by competitors. Legally protecting ideas and innovations through patents, trademarks, and copyrights is fundamental to maintaining a competitive advantage in the long term.

Strategic Collaborations and Cultural Adaptation

Strategic partnerships and alliances can also be a way for companies to differentiate and strengthen their market position. Through partnerships with other companies, research institutions, or governmental entities, companies can access new resources, skills, and markets, which can, in turn, open new growth and differentiation opportunities.

In the context of globalization, understanding and adapting to cultural differences are fundamental for international success. Companies entering new markets must be sensitive to local norms, values, and behaviors, adapting their products, services, and communication strategies accordingly. The ability to operate successfully in different cultural contexts can be a key differentiator in a global market.

Finally, the ability to anticipate and adapt to changes in consumer behavior, market trends, and economic and political contexts can be a distinctive element. Companies that are proactive rather than reactive, capable of successfully navigating through uncertainty and volatility, are better positioned to maintain and build their competitiveness over time.

Competitive Intelligence and Market Analysis

Competitive intelligence and market analysis represent additional fundamental dimensions within the framework of competition and differentiation. Today, companies are increasingly investing in tools and technologies enabling them to monitor competitors' moves, analyze market trends and forecasts, and gather insights from consumers. This ongoing analysis allows businesses to identify opportunities and threats, develop proactive and reactive strategies, and, consequently, maintain a competitive advantage.

Moreover, the importance of environmental and social sustainability in differentiation cannot be underestimated. Modern consumers are increasingly aware of environmental and social issues and tend to prefer companies demonstrating a commitment to sustainability. Adopting ethical business practices, investing in green initiatives, and engaging in social responsibility can not only enhance a company's image but also lead to long-term economic benefits.

Differentiation through Design and Innovation

Differentiation through design and innovation is another crucial aspect. Unique and appealing design can make a product or service distinctive in the eyes of consumers, while continuous innovation in terms of features, functionalities, and technology can maintain customer interest and generate brand loyalty. Attention to design and investment in research and development are therefore essential to build and maintain a competitive advantage.

Strong and Distinctive Brand Creation

Creating strong and distinctive brands is also vital in a saturated market. Building a recognizable, trustworthy brand associated with positive values can help differentiate a company from its competitors and establish an emotional connection with consumers. Branding strategies should be consistent and reflect the company's mission, vision, and values, contributing to creating a unique and distinctive identity.

Customer Relationship Management (CRM)

Another key element in differentiation is customer relationship management (CRM). Companies that develop strong and lasting relationships with their customers can create value through customer loyalty and positive word-of-mouth. Using advanced CRM technologies enables companies to personalize customer interactions, improve customer service, and effectively manage customer information, contributing to optimizing customer satisfaction and building long-term relationships.

Operational Flexibility and Adaptability

Operational flexibility and adaptability are also essential to maintain competitiveness in an ever-evolving market environment. Companies must be able to quickly adapt to changes in market conditions, demand fluctuations, and new opportunities. The ability to change operations, production processes, and business strategies in an agile and timely manner can be a distinctive factor in maintaining a competitive advantage. In summary, differentiation in today's business landscape is a complex task that requires attention to numerous factors, from innovation and sustainability to customer relationship management and operational flexibility. Companies that successfully navigate this complex environment and differentiate effectively are likely to thrive in the long term.

Market Positioning and SWOT Analysis

In the context of competition and differentiation, an essential role is played by companies' ability to create and maintain a strong market position. This involves clearly defining a unique value proposition that attracts and satisfies consumers' needs, thereby differentiating from competitors. Creating a distinctive value proposition can result from product superiority, excellent customer service, operational efficiency, or an innovative business model.

SWOT Analysis and Personalization

The SWOT analysis (Strengths, Weaknesses, Opportunities, Threats) is a crucial tool for companies seeking to differentiate. This analysis enables businesses to identify their internal strengths and weaknesses as well as external opportunities and threats, facilitating the formulation of effective strategies to gain a competitive advantage.

Personalization in Differentiation

Personalization is another fundamental aspect of differentiation. In an increasingly crowded market, offering personalized products and services can help companies meet specific customer needs, build closer relationships, and increase brand loyalty. Digital technologies such as artificial intelligence and data analysis are valuable tools to enable companies to scale and efficiently personalize offerings.

Key Element: Transparency

Another key element is transparency. In an era where consumers are increasingly informed and demanding, companies must be transparent about their business practices, the source of materials, production processes, and environmental impact. Transparency can strengthen consumer trust, improve a company's reputation, and contribute to building an ethical and responsible brand.

Extending Differentiation to the Online World

The importance of differentiation extends to the online world. Digital presence, online marketing, social media, and e-commerce have become indispensable channels to reach consumers, promote products and services, and build brand awareness. A well-planned and integrated digital strategy can expand a company's reach, enhance customer engagement, and drive conversions, contributing to the long-term success of the enterprise.

Strategic Alliances and Partnerships

Strategic alliances and partnerships can also contribute to differentiation. Collaborating with other companies, research institutions, or non-profit organizations allows businesses to access new skills, technologies, or markets, share resources and risks, and develop innovative products or services. Partnerships can be an effective means to gain a competitive advantage and differentiate in the market.

Price as a Decisive Factor

Lastly, but not less important, price remains a decisive factor in competition. An optimized pricing strategy can influence consumer perceived value, attract specific market segments, and influence market share. Whether adopting a premium pricing strategy, penetration, or discounts, striking the right balance between price and value is crucial for differentiation and commercial success.

In conclusion, competitive strategies and differentiation are multifaceted and interconnected, requiring a holistic and dynamic approach from companies to adapt, innovate, and thrive in an increasingly complex and competitive business environment.

Centrality of Competition and Differentiation

Competition and differentiation in today's business landscape are central and fundamental concepts for the success and growth of a company. An organization's ability to stand out in a saturated market is intrinsically linked to its capacity to understand market dynamics, anticipate consumer needs, and constantly innovate.

Dynamic Nature of Differentiation

In conclusion, it's vital to emphasize that differentiation is not a static but a dynamic process. Companies must be ready to adapt and reformulate their differentiation strategies in response to changing market conditions, shifts in consumer behaviors, and the evolution of technology and innovation. This demands continuous market analysis, a deep understanding of their consumer target, and a constant commitment to product innovation and improvement.

Brand Consistency and Customer Experience

Furthermore, the effectiveness of differentiation strategies is closely related to brand consistency and the quality of the customer experience.

Companies must ensure that every touchpoint with the customer reflects and reinforces their brand identity and values, thus creating a consistent and distinctive experience that meets and surpasses customer expectations.

Sustainability as a Key Differentiator

Sustainability has become a key factor in differentiation. Companies are increasingly called to demonstrate environmental, social, and economic responsibility, and those integrating sustainable practices into their business models can gain a significant competitive advantage. Sustainability is no longer just a "nice to have" but has become a necessity and an expectation from consumers, investors, and stakeholders.

Global Context and Adaptability

The importance of differentiation is even more accentuated in a global context, where companies not only compete with local rivals but also with international players. The ability to adapt and respond to cultural, legal, and market differences is crucial for international success and requires a well-thought-out and culturally sensitive differentiation strategy.

Continuous Competitive Analysis

Finally, continuous competitive analysis and monitoring are essential to identify new differentiation opportunities and promptly react to competitive threats. Companies must remain vigilant, be prepared to learn from their competitors, and adjust their strategies to maintain and strengthen their market position. These reflections conclude the analysis on the topic of competition and differentiation, underlining the importance of a strategic, innovative, and holistic approach to create unique and sustainable value in the contemporary business landscape.

24. SWOT Analysis in Retail

The SWOT analysis (Strengths, Weaknesses, Opportunities, Threats) is a strategic tool used to identify the strengths, weaknesses, opportunities, and threats of a company or sector. In the context of the Retail industry, this analysis can provide valuable insights into market dynamics and formulate effective strategies. Here is an example of a SWOT analysis for Retail:

1. Strengths:

- **Economies of Scale:** Retail can leverage economies of scale due to large purchasing volumes, reducing costs, and offering competitive prices to consumers.

- **Product Variety:** A wide range of available products satisfies a broad customer base and swiftly adapts to market needs.
- **Widespread Presence:** The extensive network of retail stores makes them easily accessible to consumers.

2. Weaknesses:

- **Reduced Margins:** Price competition may erode profit margins, making the sector sensitive to economic fluctuations.
- **Supplier Dependency:** High purchase volumes can create dependency on certain suppliers, making Retail vulnerable to supply problems.
- **Reputation Risks:** Quality issues or scandals can damage the reputation of Retail chains, leading to long-term consequences.

3. Opportunities:

- **E-commerce:** E-commerce development offers new sales and customer loyalty opportunities.
- **Sustainability:** Integrating sustainable practices into the supply chain can create a competitive advantage and attract conscientious consumers.
- **Offer Personalization:** Using technologies such as data analysis can enable personalized offerings and enhance the customer experience.

4. Threats:

- **Online Competition:** The growing popularity of e-commerce platforms poses a serious threat to traditional retailers.
- **Changes in Buying Behavior:** Consumer habit evolution can influence the demand for Retail products and services.
- **Economic Fluctuations:** Economic crises or uncertainties may reduce consumer purchasing power and negatively impact sales.

This SWOT analysis highlights the challenges and opportunities that the Retail industry faces in an ever-evolving market. Understanding these factors is fundamental to formulating strategies that leverage opportunities and mitigate risks, ensuring sector growth and sustainability.

In a context characterized by rapid changes and innovations, Retail must be prepared to reinterpret its strategies based on a dynamic SWOT analysis that is attentive to new trends. A key element in this scenario is digitalization. Digital technologies, from big data to blockchain, are altering distribution dynamics, offering new tools to optimize the supply chain, enhance customer interaction, and increase operational efficiency.

Another consideration is the importance of Corporate Social Responsibility. Retail companies can find a true strength in ethical and sustainable behavior. Consumers are increasingly mindful of the environmental and social impact of their purchased products, and distribution chains that promote responsible practices can earn consumer trust and loyalty.

Diversification of Offerings: Diversifying product ranges and considering additional services, such as home delivery, loyalty programs, or partnerships with other companies, contributes to creating a unique and engaging shopping experience for the customer.

Equally important is the ability to anticipate and adapt to demographic and socio-cultural changes. The evolution of consumer preferences and needs, as well as the emergence of new market segments, requires a continual revision of assortments and marketing strategies. For example, the growing demand for organic, ethical, or local products presents an opportunity for Retail to position itself as a promoter of conscious and sustainable choices.

Human Resource Management: Training and motivating staff are crucial to ensuring quality service and developing key digital, commercial, and relational skills. A qualified and satisfied team not only contributes to operational success but also strengthens the company's image and reputation.

The Challenge of Online Competition

The Retail sector faces increasing competition from new players in the online market. E-commerce platforms are gaining market shares by capitalizing on convenience, speed, and customized offerings. To counter this trend, it's crucial to invest in omnichannel solutions that integrate the online and offline shopping experience and in customer loyalty and engagement strategies.

Legislative Challenges and Regulatory Impacts

Additionally, the SWOT analysis should consider legislative and regulatory challenges. Regulations concerning food safety, labeling, data protection, and consumer rights are constantly evolving and require ongoing monitoring and proactive adaptation of business practices. Compliance with regulations is not only a legal obligation but can also become a differentiation factor and a competitive advantage, especially concerning transparency and responsibility towards consumers and society.

Personalization of the Shopping Experience

Within the Retail sector, personalized shopping experiences emerge as a key factor. Customers want to feel recognized and valued, and with artificial intelligence and behavioral data, companies have the opportunity to offer tailor-made products and services, strengthening the consumer bond. This opens up new possibilities for value creation but also presents challenges in terms of data privacy and security.

Logistical Efficiency

Beyond personalization, logistical efficiency is another critical point. Optimizing merchandise flows, warehouse management, and reducing delivery times significantly affect operational effectiveness and customer satisfaction. Implementing innovative technologies like drones, robots, and the Internet of Things (IoT) can improve logistics management and reduce costs.

Environmental Sustainability

In this landscape, environmental sustainability gains increasing relevance. Product life cycles, waste reduction, and the use of eco-friendly materials are central issues in consumer perception and a company's image. Initiatives promoting the circular economy and limiting environmental impact can translate into a competitive advantage and increased customer loyalty.

Resilience to External Shocks

Resilience to external shocks is another dimension to explore. Events such as pandemics, economic crises, or natural disasters can have significant repercussions on the distribution sector. The ability to anticipate, manage, and adapt to such situations is crucial to ensure operational continuity and maintain the trust of customers and business partners.

Collaboration with Startups and Ethical Business Practices

Collaboration with startups and innovative small businesses is another relevant aspect. Incubating innovative ideas and solutions, as well as creating synergies with young enterprises, can accelerate the innovation process and pave the way for new products, services, and business models. Additionally, ethics and transparency in business practices and relationships with suppliers and customers are becoming increasingly critical factors.

Global Competition and Cultural Adaptation

Lastly, competition with international markets and the ability to adapt to diverse cultures and regulations influence the strategy and competitive position of Retail companies. Knowledge of local dynamics, flexibility, and innovation are essential for successful operations in a globalized context.

The Role of Digitalization

Digitalization is a key element in the evolution of Retail. Beyond e-commerce, the use of digital platforms, mobile applications, and augmented reality is changing how customers interact with companies and make purchases. This digital transformation not only expands sales opportunities but also allows the collection of valuable consumer behavior data, enabling in-depth analysis and real-time adaptation of marketing strategies.

The Role of Social Media and Technology in Retail

The significance of social media in building brand image and customer relationships continues to grow. Online reviews, comments, and shares significantly influence consumers' purchasing decisions. Managing online reputation and proactive community engagement have become essential skills for Retail companies.

Furthermore, the evolution of blockchain technologies offers new perspectives in product traceability and transaction management. This technology can ensure greater transparency and security, reduce fraud risks, and enhance supply chain efficiency.

Focus on Local Products and Employee Training

The increasing attention towards local products and the origin of raw materials represents another ongoing trend. Consumers are more informed and sensitive to ethical and environmental issues, demanding products that reflect these values. Certification of origin, zero-kilometer production, and the promotion of local typical products can be a significant differentiation factor.

In this scenario, employee training and updating become crucial. The speed of technological change and the complexity of new challenges require increasingly specific skills and a constant ability to learn and adapt. Investing in staff training and promoting a culture open to innovation are fundamental steps to remain competitive.

Diversification and Inclusivity

Another aspect is diversifying offerings. Beyond product sales, Retail companies are exploring new business models such as service sales, organizing events and experiences, and creating partnerships with other companies to offer integrated packages and enhance their brand. Finally, the theme of inclusivity and diversity is increasingly central to business strategies. Retail, by its nature of interfacing with a diverse public, has the responsibility and opportunity to promote values of inclusivity and respect for differences, both within the organization and in relationships with customers and the community.

SWOT Analysis in Retail

In conclusion, a SWOT analysis of Retail requires careful consideration of various key elements influencing the sector. In terms of strengths, the capacity to adapt to new technologies, broad market coverage, and diversified offerings significantly contribute to the success of companies in the sector. The effective implementation of e-commerce strategies and the intelligent use of customer data can also be seen as strengths.

Regarding weaknesses, Retail can be vulnerable to rapid changes in consumer behavior and economic fluctuations. Human resource management and staff training are areas that require continuous attention to ensure employees can meet customer needs in an ever-evolving environment.

There are numerous and varied opportunities. The evolution of digital technologies and the growing importance of sustainability and corporate ethics offer new possibilities for growth and differentiation. Expanding into new markets and creating strategic partnerships can open new horizons and contribute to long-term success.

However, threats should not be underestimated. Competition is increasingly fierce and global, with new players constantly entering the market. Regulations may impose additional restrictions and obligations, while economic and health crises, such as the one caused by COVID-19, put companies' resilience to the test.

In essence, Retail faces unique challenges and opportunities. The ability to anticipate future trends, adapt quickly, and maintain a strong customer bond will be crucial for long-term success. The integration of innovation and tradition, global and local, efficiency and sustainability, will be the pillars on which to build future strategies for companies in this sector.

25. Case Studies and Success Stories

When exploring case studies and success stories in the business world, we can identify several examples of companies that have distinguished themselves through innovative strategies, adaptability, and forward-thinking entrepreneurship.

1. Apple Inc.: Apple is often cited as an emblematic example of innovation and design. The company has revolutionized various sectors, such as music, telecommunications, and computing, through iconic products like the iPod, iPhone, and MacBook. Emphasis on design quality, user experience, and an integrated ecosystem of products and services has contributed to its global success.

2. Amazon.com: Starting as an online bookstore, Amazon has become the world's largest e-commerce platform, offering a wide range of products and services. The company has diversified by entering sectors such as cloud computing with Amazon Web Services and digital entertainment with Amazon Prime Video.

3. Tesla, Inc.: Tesla has revolutionized the automotive industry by introducing high-performance electric vehicles. Elon Musk's vision and continuous innovation in terms of technology, design, and sustainability have positioned Tesla as a leader in the electric mobility sector.

4. Patagonia: This outdoor clothing company is renowned for its commitment to sustainability and social responsibility. Patagonia has incorporated ethical principles into every aspect of its business, from using recycled materials to promoting environmental conservation, earning consumer loyalty and creating a sustainable business model.

5. Airbnb: Airbnb has reinvented the concept of tourist accommodation, allowing individuals to rent their homes to travelers worldwide. The innovative approach and user-friendly platform have helped create a global market, offering an alternative to traditional forms of accommodation and generating new economic opportunities.

6. Beyond Meat: Beyond Meat is a successful example in the food industry. The company has developed plant-based meat alternatives, responding to the growing demand for more sustainable and healthy food options. Its ability to replicate the taste and texture of meat has attracted consumers and investors, positioning the company as a pioneer in the alternative protein market.

These cases illustrate how innovation, strategic vision, and ethical commitment can contribute to a company's success. The lessons learned from these stories can offer inspiration and guidance for entrepreneurs and managers aspiring to create value in the contemporary business context.

Continuing to Explore Case Studies and Success Stories

In addition, it is essential to observe how some companies have used their resources, skills, and capabilities to overcome obstacles and achieve ambitious goals.

1. Spotify: The music streaming platform has changed the way we consume music by introducing a subscription-based model that provides access to an extensive music library. Personalization and discovering new tracks have become the core of the user experience, with playlists and algorithm-based recommendations.

2. Zara: Zara's fast-fashion approach has revolutionized the fashion industry. The speed of bringing new products to the market, responding in real-time to trends, has made Zara one of the most recognized and successful fashion brands globally.

3. Netflix: Starting as a DVD-by-mail rental service, Netflix has transformed into a streaming giant, producing original content and acquiring exclusive rights to films and TV series. Personalization and a variety of content have captured a global audience.

4. Shopify: This e-commerce platform has allowed countless small businesses to sell online, providing the necessary tools to manage a virtual store. Ease of use and flexibility have contributed to Shopify's rapid growth.

5. Slack: Slack has transformed communication within organizations, introducing a new way to collaborate and share information. The intuitive interface and the ability to integrate other applications have made Slack an essential tool for many businesses.

6. Square: Founded by Jack Dorsey, co-founder of Twitter, Square has made electronic payments more accessible to small businesses. The mobile payment solution has eliminated the need for expensive POS terminals, facilitating secure and efficient transactions.

7. Palantir: Specializing in data analysis, Palantir has developed powerful platforms for processing and analyzing vast amounts of information, helping organizations and governments make informed decisions and act more effectively.

These companies represent a wide variety of sectors and business models, but they all share the ability to innovate, adapt, and capitalize on emerging opportunities. By examining their paths and strategies adopted, one can gain deeper insights into achieving success in an ever-evolving market.

In Conclusion: Understanding Success Stories

Concluding, the analysis of case studies and success stories is a crucial exercise to deeply comprehend how different companies, operating in various sectors, have leveraged innovation, market strategies, and adaptability to emerge and thrive in competitive and ever-evolving markets. One of the key aspects that emerged is the importance of innovation and the ability to anticipate or quickly respond to market changes and consumer needs. Companies like Netflix and Spotify, for example, have revolutionized entire sectors thanks to their capacity to offer new consumption models and personalized services, becoming undisputed leaders in their respective fields.

Another critical factor is the ability to create and maintain a competitive advantage, which can come from operational efficiency, product quality, brand identity, or a combination of these elements. Zara, for example, has built its success on the efficiency of its supply chain and the ability to quickly interpret market trends, features that have enabled the company to stand out in a highly competitive sector.

Additionally, attention to customer needs and the ability to provide effective and convenient solutions are distinguishing elements of successful companies. Shopify and Square, for example, responded to specific market needs by offering intuitive and accessible services, facilitating entry into the electronic market and digital payments for small businesses and merchants.

Resilience and adaptability in the face of challenges and market changes are also essential. Companies must navigate through crises, such as the COVID-19 pandemic, and seize emerging opportunities by adjusting their business and operational models based on new circumstances and changing consumer needs.

Finally, the examination of these success stories highlights the importance of strategic vision and strong leadership. The ability to anticipate future trends, make informed decisions, and motivate and guide human resources are essential skills to build and maintain a successful enterprise in a global and rapidly evolving context.

In summary, the detailed study of these success stories provides valuable lessons and insights that can guide entrepreneurs, managers, and professionals in formulating and implementing effective strategies to achieve success in the contemporary business context.

26. Business Failures and Lessons Learned

Examining business failures and lessons learned, it's evident that companies face numerous challenges and difficulties that can lead to negative outcomes if not properly managed. However, even in failure, there are valuable lessons to be learned that can inform and guide future entrepreneurial efforts.

One critical aspect that emerges is the importance of sound financial management. Companies like Lehman Brothers experienced a devastating collapse due to risky financial practices and lack of transparency, underscoring the importance of financial prudence and regulatory compliance. The lessons learned from such failures have led to regulatory reforms and greater awareness of the importance of risk management in the financial sector.

Understanding and responding to consumer needs is another key theme. Blockbuster, once a leader in the film sales and rental market, experienced rapid decline due to its inability to adapt to the rise of digitization and online streaming services. Its story serves as a warning for companies about the importance of staying current with technological advancements and changes in consumer behavior.

Adaptability and flexibility are essential qualities that can help companies overcome unexpected challenges and capitalize on new opportunities. Kodak, for example, despite being a pioneer in photographic technology, struggled with the transition to the digital age and eventually filed for bankruptcy. Its story highlights the need for continuous innovation and readiness to renew to stay competitive.

Furthermore, human resource management is a fundamental factor for a company's success. Organizations that fail to motivate, engage, and value their workforce may experience productivity issues, turnover, and dissatisfaction, ultimately affecting business performance negatively.

Finally, the lack of a clear vision and strategy can be fatal for businesses. Companies must have a clear understanding of their long-term objectives, strengths, weaknesses, and the markets they operate in. Inadequate planning and analysis can lead to wrong decisions and loss of market opportunities.

In conclusion, business failures provide significant learning opportunities. Analyzing the causes of failures and understanding the lessons learned can help entrepreneurs and managers avoid similar mistakes, develop more resilient and adaptive strategies, and build stronger and more sustainable businesses over time.

Continuing the Exploration of Failures and Lessons Learned

As exploration continues in the realm of failures and lessons learned, it becomes evident how the external environment and market context play a significant role in determining a company's success or failure. The impact of macroeconomic factors, legislative changes, competitive dynamics, and the evolution of consumer preferences can profoundly alter the landscape in which a company operates, making accurate environmental analysis essential.

The 2008 economic crisis highlighted how vulnerability to external economic shocks can have devastating effects on companies, regardless of their size or sector. The crisis underscored the importance of maintaining a strong balance sheet, diversifying income sources, and having contingency plans in place to address periods of economic uncertainty.

The global health emergency of COVID-19 further emphasized the need for companies to be resilient and flexible. Many organizations were forced to rethink their business models, shift to e-commerce, and find new ways to interact with customers. This experience highlighted the importance of continuous innovation and adaptability to maintain relevance and vitality in a rapidly changing world.

Market dynamics and competition are also crucial determinants of success. Companies like Yahoo! saw their fortunes decline due to increased competition and the failure to differentiate effectively in the market. Yahoo! once dominated the world of search engines and internet services, but its inability to innovate and keep pace with market demands saw it overtaken by more agile and future-oriented competitors.

Another Key Factor: Reputation and Brand Perception

Another key factor is the reputation and perception of the brand. Companies that don't effectively manage their public image and don't proactively address customer and stakeholder concerns can suffer long-term damage to their reputation. A noteworthy case is Enron, whose lack of business ethics and unethical practices led to its collapse, resulting in lasting repercussions on public trust in companies.

Furthermore, companies must pay attention to the evolution of technologies and their impact on existing business models. The rise of blockchain, artificial intelligence, and the Internet of Things (IoT) is revolutionizing entire sectors, and companies failing to adopt and integrate these technologies risk being left behind.

Sustainability is another increasingly important consideration. Companies that do not adopt sustainable practices and do not consider the environmental and social impact of their operations may face growing risks in terms of regulatory compliance and public perception. The increasing commitment to sustainability by consumers, investors, and legislators makes it essential for companies to integrate sustainability into their business strategies.

Finally, understanding organizational culture and engaging employees are essential aspects of building and maintaining a successful organization. Talent management, skill development, and creating an inclusive and motivating work environment are all factors contributing to improved productivity and employee satisfaction, and therefore to the long-term resilience and success of the company. Considering all these dynamics, it's clear that companies must adopt a holistic and multifaceted approach to navigate effectively in today's complex business landscape and continuously learn from past challenges and failures.

Exploring Risk Management

Another aspect to explore when analyzing failures and lessons learned is risk management. Companies that don't proactively identify, evaluate, and mitigate risks can find themselves exposed to significant losses and irreparable damages. For example, the failure to consider risks associated with climate change, such as extreme weather events and stricter regulations, can have direct and indirect impacts on business operations, the supply chain, and the company's reputation itself.

Simultaneously, legal and compliance issues have become increasingly complex, requiring companies to stay updated on the laws and regulations in the markets they operate in. Non-compliance can lead to financial penalties, legal actions, and damage to reputation, thus compromising stakeholder trust and negatively impacting the company's performance. Additionally, in the digital age, cybersecurity has become a priority for companies of every size and sector. Increasing cyber-attacks and data breaches put sensitive customer and company information at risk, with financial and reputational consequences. Companies that do not adequately invest in cybersecurity and implement preventive measures may suffer significant losses.

Another critical aspect is managing customer relations. Customer dissatisfaction and inefficiencies in handling complaints can lead to customer loss and negative reviews, affecting the company's image and its ability to attract new customers. Companies that do not place the customer at the center of their strategy and do not invest in customer service and relationships may face difficulties in retaining and expanding their market share.

Adapting to Market Changes
The ability to anticipate and adapt to market changes is crucial. Continuous innovation and anticipating market trends allow companies to remain competitive and create products and services that meet the growing expectations of consumers. Companies that fail to innovate and adapt can lose ground to more agile and responsive competitors.
In addition, financial management and strategic planning are key elements for stability and business growth. Companies that do not effectively manage financial resources and do not proactively plan may encounter difficulties in sustaining operations and investing in new opportunities.
Finally, corporate culture and employee engagement continue to be critical factors for

long-term success. Companies that do not value their employees and do not promote a positive work environment may experience high turnover, low motivation, and reduced productivity.

In summary, carefully considering and analyzing all these elements and learning from past experiences is essential to avoid failures and ensure the resilience and success of companies in the current dynamic and competitive context.

Handling Internal Conflicts

Another key element in failures and lessons learned is a company's ability to manage and prevent internal conflicts. Disputes among team members, between different departments, or between leadership and staff can erode corporate cohesion, decrease productivity, and contribute to a toxic work environment. Companies that learn from these situations invest in conflict management training and promote communication and collaboration at all levels.

Sustainability and Its Importance

Sustainability is another central theme in today's landscape. Companies that do not integrate sustainable practices into their business models may face increasing pressure from stakeholders, investors, and consumers. The lack of sustainable initiatives can also limit access to new markets and reduce the company's competitiveness. Lessons learned in this area drive companies to

adopt long-term strategies to reduce
environmental impact and promote social
responsibility.

Digitalization

Digitalization is another fundamental aspect. In
the current context, characterized by rapid
technological advancements, companies that do
not embrace digitalization can lag behind. Lack
of digital skills, resistance to change, and
insufficient investment in technology can limit a
company's ability to compete and innovate.
Learning from these challenges encourages
companies to develop digital skills and adopt
advanced technological solutions.

Human Capital Management

Furthermore, human capital management is
essential. Companies that do not value and
develop talent may face difficulties in recruiting
and retaining top talent. The absence of
professional development plans, lack of career
opportunities, and pay inequity can fuel
employee dissatisfaction and negatively impact
company performance.

Strategic Flexibility

Strategic flexibility is another crucial factor.
Companies must be able to quickly adapt to
unforeseen market changes, new opportunities,
or emerging challenges. Rigid planning and a
lack of agility can make it difficult for a company

to navigate in an evolving business environment and can lead to financial losses and failures. Finally, the importance of emotional intelligence in leadership cannot be underestimated. Leaders who lack empathy, effective communication, and motivation for their teams can contribute to employee disengagement and a decline in morale, which can, in turn, negatively impact business outcomes.

All these considerations highlight the complexity of business management and the importance of continuously learning from challenges and failures to build resilient and successful organizations.

Concluding Thoughts on "Failures and Lessons Learned"

The point about "Failures and Lessons Learned" is of vital importance for any company aspiring to grow and thrive in an ever-evolving business environment. Organizations must take a proactive approach to identify and analyze failures, welcoming these moments as valuable opportunities to learn and improve.

Attention to managing internal conflicts, implementing sustainable practices, embracing digitalization, valuing human capital, strategic flexibility, and developing emotional intelligence in leadership are all key areas that, if overlooked, can lead to business failures. Conversely, if handled carefully, they can become pillars of success and growth.

Companies must also develop an organizational culture that promotes open and honest communication, creating an environment where employees feel valued and heard. Creating an inclusive and supportive work environment can help prevent disengagement and improve productivity and employee satisfaction.

A systematic and well-structured approach to risk management is also indispensable. The ability to anticipate, identify, and mitigate risks can help companies successfully navigate market challenges and avoid costly mistakes. Moreover, a deep understanding of the market, competitors, and customer needs is essential for developing effective strategies and adapting to the ever-evolving dynamics of the industry.

Finally, it's essential that the lessons learned are integrated into the company's DNA through continuous training, process reviews, and creating feedback mechanisms. Only by adopting a holistic approach to organizational learning can companies hope to transform failures into opportunities, promote innovation, improve competitiveness, and build a sustainable and prosperous future.

In summary, reflecting on failures and learning from the lessons derived are indispensable

components for business progress. They
represent the key to evolving, adapting, and
thriving in an increasingly complex and
challenging entrepreneurial world.

27. Role of Emerging Technologies (Blockchain, AI, etc.)

- The role of emerging technologies such as Blockchain, Artificial Intelligence (AI), Internet of Things (IoT), and others is fundamental in shaping the future of business and shaping new operational and market paradigms. These technologies have become engines of innovation, creating unprecedented opportunities for businesses in various sectors.
- **Blockchain**: Blockchain offers transparency, security, and decentralization. In many sectors, from finance to healthcare, this technology allows tracking transactions and ensuring data integrity. Companies are exploring its use to enhance the supply chain, reduce costs, and prevent fraud.

- **Artificial Intelligence (AI)**: AI can analyze complex data, recognize patterns, and make decisions. It's used to optimize business processes, improve customer service through chatbots and virtual assistants, detect fraud, and predict market trends. AI can also support product innovation and offer personalization.
- **Internet of Things (IoT)**: IoT connects physical devices to the Internet, enabling communication among themselves and with users. This connectivity is revolutionizing sectors like manufacturing, agriculture, and healthcare through real-time monitoring, predictive maintenance, and large-scale data collection.
- **Augmented and Virtual Reality (AR/VR)**: AR and VR are finding applications in training, marketing, product design, and support services. For instance, they allow customers to view products in a virtual environment before purchase or technicians to receive remote assistance.
- **5G**: The fifth generation of mobile technology is enabling real-time communication and high-speed data processing, giving rise to new opportunities in IoT, autonomous vehicles, telemedicine, and more.
- **Robotics and Automation**: The adoption of robots and automation solutions is improving operational efficiency, reducing costs, and

eliminating human errors. Collaborative robotics, in particular, allows greater interaction and cooperation between humans and machines.

- Emerging technologies are redefining how companies operate, compete, and create value. The ability to adopt and integrate these technologies can determine success or failure in the current market. However, it's essential for companies to address the ethical, privacy, and security challenges associated with adopting these technologies to ensure sustainable and responsible progress.

- **The Role of Emerging Technologies in Various Sectors**

- The role of emerging technologies is deeply rooted in the development and progress of multiple industrial and commercial sectors. The potentials offered by these technologies are immense and are expanding in innovative and revolutionary ways.

- **Cloud Computing**: Cloud Computing has changed how companies store, access, and share data. It offers scalability, flexibility, and cost savings, enabling organizations to respond quickly to market needs and implement new solutions.

- **Big Data and Analytics**: Big Data analysis enables companies to extract valuable information from data to optimize operations, make informed decisions, and create personalized products or services. Analytics tools are essential for understanding market trends and consumer behavior.

- **Cybersecurity**: With increasing digitalization, information security has become a central concern. Cybersecurity solutions are essential to protect sensitive data, prevent cyber-attacks, and ensure operational continuity.
- **Green Technologies**: The adoption of sustainable and green technologies is becoming crucial to reduce the ecological footprint of companies. Renewable energies, biodegradable materials, and energy-efficient solutions are just some of the innovations driving the transition to a green economy.

• **Biotech and Nanotech:** Biotechnologies and nanotechnologies are bringing significant changes in fields such as medicine, agriculture, and material production. These technologies can contribute to the development of advanced medical treatments, more nutritious foods, and stronger materials.

• **Additive Manufacturing:** 3D printing is revolutionizing manufacturing, allowing the creation of complex objects, mass customization, and reducing production times and costs.

• **Digital Twin:** Digital Twin technology creates a digital replica of a physical object or system. This allows monitoring, analyzing, and simulating situations in a virtual environment, optimizing maintenance and resource management.

Incorporating these technologies into business strategies is not just a proactive choice, it's becoming an imperative. Companies must remain vigilant and quickly adapt to technological evolution to maintain competitiveness and meet growing customer expectations. Furthermore, it's important to consider the ethical and social implications of these technologies and promote a responsible and inclusive approach to technological development.

• **Artificial Intelligence (AI) and Machine Learning:** These technologies are revolutionizing numerous sectors with their ability to learn and make decisions. In retail, AI is used for predictive sales analysis, price optimization, inventory management, and customer assistance through chatbots. Machine learning is particularly critical for pattern recognition and consumer behavior analysis.

• **Blockchain:** Blockchain has applications well beyond cryptocurrencies. In the retail sector, it can be used to trace the origin and provenance of products, ensuring transparency and consumer trust. Additionally, it can streamline transactions and reduce costs through smart contracts.

• **Augmented and Virtual Reality (AR/VR):** AR and VR are changing the shopping experience by allowing customers to view products in a three-dimensional environment or virtually try on clothing and accessories. These technologies also contribute to staff training and store design.

• **Internet of Things (IoT):** IoT enables the connection of physical devices to the network, collecting data and offering new interaction possibilities. In retail, it can be used to monitor product storage conditions, manage store lighting and air conditioning, and offer personalized services to customers through mobile devices.

• **Automation and Robotics:** Process automation and the use of robots are reducing management times and costs. Robots can be employed for restocking, inventory, and delivery, while automation can streamline cashier operations and customer service.

• **5G:** The fifth generation of mobile technology is improving the speed and reliability of internet connections. This is crucial to support the implementation of advanced technologies like IoT, AR/VR, and automation, as well as improving the online and in-store shopping experience.

• **Circular Economy:** Adopting circular business models is essential to reduce the environmental impact of retail. This includes recycling, reusing, waste reduction, and promoting responsible consumption.

Staying updated on technological advancements and effectively integrating them into business strategies is crucial for the long-term sustainability and success in the retail sector. This also involves the need to invest in employee training and skill development and consider the social and ethical implications of adopting new technologies.

• **Big Data and Analytics:** Using Big Data and Analytics is crucial to analyze large volumes of data in real-time. This allows retailers to obtain valuable insights into consumer buying behaviors, preferences, and trends, enabling the customization of offers and services, improving inventory management, and optimizing prices.

• **Cybersecurity:** With the rise of digitalization, protecting customer data and transactions becomes increasingly crucial. Investing in robust cybersecurity solutions is essential to prevent data breaches and ensure customer trust.

• **E-Commerce and Online Platforms:** The expansion of e-commerce platforms is an unstoppable trend, with more consumers preferring to shop online. Retail must adapt to this reality by improving online presence, optimizing logistics, and integrating omnichannel solutions.

• **Sustainability and Social Responsibility:** The adoption of sustainable and responsible practices is increasingly demanded by consumers. This involves using renewable energy sources, reducing plastic use, implementing corporate social responsibility programs, and promoting eco-friendly products.

• **Drones and Autonomous Vehicles:** The use of drones and autonomous vehicles for delivery is becoming more concrete. These technologies can reduce shipping costs, increase efficiency, and decrease the environmental impact of deliveries.

• **Personalization and CRM:** Customer Relationship Management (CRM) solutions and personalization are essential for building lasting relationships with customers. This includes loyalty programs, personalized offers, and direct communication to increase customer retention and the value of the lifetime value.

• **Digital Twin:** Digital Twin technology allows the creation of a virtual replica of a product, process, or service. This helps in simulation, analysis, and control, allowing the testing of new strategies and optimization of operations without interfering with the physical system.

• **3D Printing:** 3D printing offers new possibilities in production and product customization, reducing production costs and times, and offering tailored solutions to customers.

• **Digital Payments and Cryptocurrencies:** The increase in digital payments and the introduction of cryptocurrencies as a method of payment introduce new transaction methods, reducing costs and increasing transaction security and speed.

These trends and technological evolutions outline an ever-changing landscape where retail must navigate wisely to remain competitive and meet growing consumer expectations. Adaptability and innovation are therefore essential keys to success in the industry.

The assessment of the impact and implementation of emerging technologies in the retail sector is crucial for its future development and resilience. In conclusion, it is appropriate to highlight some key aspects and suggest strategies for the future:

1. **Adaptability and Innovation:** The speed at which new technologies emerge implies that retail must remain agile and adaptable. Continuous innovation, the adoption of new technological solutions, and anticipation of trends can create a substantial competitive advantage.

2. **Investment and Training:** Investment in new technologies is fundamental, but it is equally important to invest in staff training. This ensures that employees can effectively use the new technologies, optimizing the benefits and reducing risks.

3. **Security and Ethics:** While exploring the potential of new technologies, data security and consideration of ethical implications are fundamental. Consumer trust can be easily compromised and must be safeguarded through responsible and transparent practices.

4. **Sustainability:** Sustainability is a key driver in modern consumer behavior. Integrating technologies that contribute to environmental and social sustainability can not only improve the company's image but also open up new market opportunities.

5. **Collaboration and Partnerships:** Forming partnerships with technology startups, research institutions, and other companies can accelerate the adoption of emerging technologies. This collaborative approach can also help share the risks and opportunities associated with innovation.

6. **Continuous Analysis and Evaluation:** The implementation of any new technology should be

accompanied by a continuous analysis of its impact and effectiveness. This allows real-time adjustments and ensures that the investment generates the desired return.

7. **Customer Experience:** Finally, every adoption of emerging technology should be evaluated in terms of its impact on the customer experience. Technology should serve to enhance the customer's interaction with the company, meet their needs, and exceed their expectations.

In summary, while emerging technologies offer immense opportunities for retail, it is essential that the adoption of these technologies is carefully planned, ethically responsible, and focused on creating value for both the company and the customers. The future of retail is inextricably linked to its successful integration of technological innovations in an increasingly dynamic and customer-oriented landscape.

28. Impact on the Local Community

The impact of retail on the local community is multifaceted and of considerable importance. To fully evaluate such impact, it is essential to explore various aspects including the local economy, employment, the environment, and social fabric.

1. **Local Economy:** Retail can significantly influence the local economy. On one hand, the arrival of large retail chains can increase competition, sometimes putting small local businesses at risk. On the other hand, it can stimulate the economy by creating jobs and increasing customer flow in the area.
2. **Employment:** Job creation is one of the most immediate impacts. However, it's important to assess the quality of employment offered in terms of wages, working conditions, and professional growth opportunities.
3. **Environment:** The environmental impact of retail is significant. Choices related to sustainability, waste management, resource use, and CO_2 emissions affect the local environment and, ultimately, the community's quality of life.
4. **Social Integration:** Retail can contribute to the social fabric by providing meeting spaces and services to the community. Corporate Social Responsibility (CSR) initiatives can improve community life and create a positive connection between the business and local residents.
5. **Access to Products and Services:** The variety and availability of products and services can increase, improving access to diverse goods

at competitive prices. This can be particularly
advantageous in underserved areas.

6. **Impact on Local Trade:** Competition with
   small local retailers is a critical issue. While some
   local businesses may suffer, others may benefit
   from increased traffic in the area.

7. **Tax Contribution:** Large companies
   significantly contribute to local tax revenues,
   which can be reinvested in public services and
   infrastructure, benefiting the entire community.

8. **Culture and Local Identity:** The presence of
   retail can influence local culture and identity. On
   one hand, it can lead to standardization and the
   loss of local specificity; on the other hand, it can
   offer opportunities to promote local products and
   traditions.

In conclusion, the impact of retail on the local
community is complex and multifaceted. It's
essential for both public decision-makers and
businesses to be aware of the consequences of
their activities and to operate responsibly and
sustainably to create a balance between economic
development and community well-being.
Dialogue, collaboration, and commitment to
sustainability and social well-being form the
basis of a constructive relationship between retail
and the local community.
The impact of retail on the local community is a
rich and multidimensional theme that extends

well beyond the aforementioned points. It interweaves with socio-economic, environmental, and cultural dynamics, reflecting the multiple facets of community life.

9. **Consumer Education:** Retail plays a key role in educating consumers about the products they purchase. Information labels, awareness campaigns, and loyalty programs can influence buying habits and consumers' awareness of sustainability and responsible consumption.

10. **Urban Development:** The localization of large shopping centers can determine significant changes in urban fabric and mobility dynamics. Urbanization, increased traffic, and changes to regulatory plans can alter urban balance and the livability of cities.

11. **Supplier Relations:** Relationships between retail and local suppliers are fundamental. Adopting fair business practices and promoting local products can stimulate the local economy and support small-scale production.

12. **Innovation and Technology:** The introduction of innovative technologies in operational processes and sales strategies can have repercussions on the local community, fostering innovation and creating new professional opportunities.

13. **Public Health:** Retail influences public health through the availability and promotion of healthy

foods, compliance with hygiene standards, and awareness of healthy lifestyles.

14. **Social Inclusion:** The accessibility and availability of goods and services can contribute to social inclusion, particularly in disadvantaged areas, where the presence of retail can bridge gaps in commercial offerings.

15. **Governance and Regulation:** Interaction with local authorities and compliance with regulations influence the impact on the community. Collaboration with public entities is fundamental to ensuring a harmonious integration into the local fabric.

16. **Social Responsibility:** Social responsibility initiatives, such as supporting community projects and philanthropy, can enhance the company's perception and contribute to community well-being.

17. **Tourism and Territorial Attractiveness:** The presence of large commercial facilities can attract visitors from other areas, contributing to local tourism development and the valorization of the territory.

Each listed aspect affects the relationship between retail and the local community, creating an interconnected system of opportunities and challenges. Conscious management of these dynamics is crucial to ensure a balanced and mutually beneficial coexistence.

In Conclusion: The Role of Retail in Local Communities

It is undeniable that retail plays a predominant role in shaping the socio-economic and cultural fabric of local communities. From the analysis conducted, it's clear how its activities intricately interweave with various spheres of daily and community life.

Economic Impact: Retail can act as a catalyst for local economic development, stimulating employment, fostering the growth of local businesses through partnerships, and simultaneously increasing competition. However, this impact isn't always positive; price pressure and market conditions can endanger the survival of small local businesses and alter market balance.

Urban Development: The establishment of large retail structures inevitably alters the geography of cities and communities, changing mobility dynamics and potentially triggering processes of gentrification. Hence, careful urban planning and close collaboration with local authorities are fundamental to minimize negative impacts.

Public Health and Consumer Education: Retail has the opportunity and responsibility to promote informed choices and healthy lifestyles.

Transparency, clear product labeling, and the promotion of balanced foods are all crucial aspects in this context.

Social Inclusion: Retail can build a constructive relationship with the local community by providing access to essential goods and services in disadvantaged areas, supporting integration and inclusion projects to reduce inequalities and enhance social cohesion.

Innovation, Technology, and Social Responsibility: These are strategic areas through which retail can shape its impact on the community, fostering sustainable development, creating new opportunities, and strengthening ties with the local territory.

In summary, while retail brings numerous potential benefits to local communities, the risks and challenges are not negligible. It is imperative for businesses to operate with awareness, responsibility, and genuine commitment to sustainability and the well-being of the communities in which they are situated. Only through a balanced and inclusive approach, based on dialogue and collaboration with all stakeholders, is it possible to build a harmonious and prosperous future.

29. Business Models and Competitive Strategies in Retail

Business models and competitive strategies in retail are essential to navigate a dynamic and highly competitive market. Companies in the industry adopt various approaches and strategies to differentiate themselves, attract and retain customers, and stay relevant in an ever-evolving environment.

Product Differentiation:

• Companies strive to offer unique, high-quality products, often with proprietary brands, to stand out from the competition and create their brand identity.

Competitive Pricing:

• Price positioning is crucial. Some companies adopt a cost leadership strategy by offering low-priced products, while others position themselves as premium, focusing on quality and added value.

Customer Experience:

• Investing in customer experience is vital. This includes excellent customer service, pleasant shopping environments, loyalty programs, and personalized offers.

Omnichannel and Digitalization:

• Retail is increasingly embracing omnichannel retailing, integrating online and offline shopping experiences and investing in digital platforms and emerging technologies to improve accessibility and convenience.

Sustainability and Social Responsibility:

• A growing number of consumers are attentive to sustainable and ethical practices. Companies are responding through the adoption of eco-friendly practices, offering sustainable products, and implementing social responsibility initiatives.

Innovation and Adaptability:

• Innovation is key in a rapidly changing market. Companies must be ready to adapt, experimenting with new store formats, technologies, and customer interaction methods.

Geographical Expansion and Diversification:

• Expansion into new markets and diversifying offerings allow companies to reduce risks and access new customer segments.

Partnerships and Collaborations:

• Strategic alliances, partnerships, and collaborations with other companies can open new opportunities, improve offerings, and enhance market expertise.

Operational Efficiency:

• Optimizing operations and the supply chain is essential to reduce costs, improve product availability, and provide effective customer service.

Data Analytics and Artificial Intelligence:
• Advanced use of data analytics and artificial intelligence allows a better understanding of customer behaviors, inventory optimization, and personalized marketing strategies.

In conclusion, the implementation and integration of these business models and competitive strategies are vital for the success of companies in retail. In an increasingly complex and challenging environment, the ability to innovate, adapt, and respond to consumer needs will determine long-term sustainability and growth.

Continued Exploration of New Business Models and Competitive Strategies

Companies in the retail sector continue to explore new business models and competitive strategies to stay ahead. The market environment is fluid, and consumer needs are continually evolving, demanding a proactive and innovative approach.

Vertical Integration:
• Companies are exploring vertical integration, gaining more control over the supply chain from start to finish. This not only allows for greater

product consistency and quality but also reduces costs and improves operational control.

Customer Engagement:

• Investing in customer engagement through online communities, exclusive events, and advanced loyalty programs is becoming increasingly central. Active customer engagement helps build a stronger bond with the brand, fostering loyalty and retention.

Micro-Targeting and Personalization:

• Micro-targeting techniques, based on big data analysis and machine learning, offer tailored promotions and products for individual consumers, increasing the relevance and effectiveness of marketing campaigns.

Private Brand Development:

• Creating and promoting private brands allows companies to offer exclusive products, increasing differentiation and profit margins. These products are often positioned as high-quality alternatives to national brands.

Agility and Scalability:

• The ability to scale rapidly and adapt to market changes is essential. Implementing flexible technological platforms and adopting agile methodologies can help companies respond promptly to new opportunities and challenges.

Circular Economy: The integration of circular economy principles in operations and products helps reduce environmental impact and meets the growing consumer demand for sustainable and responsible products.

Localization Strategies: Adapting offerings to local tastes and preferences can be a key success factor in new markets. This can include offering local products, personalized marketing, and adjusting in-store experiences.

Investment in R&D: Continuous investment in research and development is crucial to maintaining a competitive edge. This includes developing new products, adopting new technologies, and innovating operational processes.

Exploration of New Distribution Channels: Companies are always looking for innovative distribution channels to reach consumers. This can involve expanding into new store formats, experimenting with direct-to-consumer sales models, and collaborating with e-commerce platforms.

Consumer Education: Educating consumers about brand values, product quality, and commitment to sustainability can help build a positive reputation and stimulate demand. Through the exploration and adoption of these strategies and models, retail companies aim to navigate an evolving market, anticipate trends, meet consumer expectations, and build a sustainable and prosperous future.

Digitalization and Technology: In response to the growing prevalence of digital technologies, many companies are strengthening their online presence and developing intuitive and user-friendly apps and websites. Digitalization not only improves operational efficiency but also offers new opportunities for customer personalization and engagement through digital channels.

Sustainability and Social Responsibility: Increasing attention towards sustainability is compelling companies to reconsider their operational practices and supply chain. Adopting eco-friendly packaging, reducing carbon footprints, and supporting local social initiatives are among the strategies to build a responsible and ethical brand image.

Omnichannel Retailing: The evolution of consumer expectations has made an omnichannel approach a necessity for retailers. Combining online and offline shopping experiences aims to offer consumers greater convenience and flexibility.

Diversification of Offerings: To maintain and increase market share, companies are constantly exploring diversification opportunities. This can include expanding into new product categories, entering new market segments, or creating strategic collaborations and partnerships.

Innovation in Services: Beyond products, innovation in services is another pillar of competitive strategies. Services such as fast delivery, subscription programs, and flexible pickup options can enhance customer experience and create added value.

Focus on Health and Wellness: Aligning with the growing trends towards a healthy lifestyle, many companies are expanding their range of organic, gluten-free, vegan, and other healthy products. Educating consumers and promoting mindful food choices are becoming integral parts of marketing strategies.

Data Analysis and Consumer Insights: Access to and analysis of vast amounts of consumer data allows companies to better understand habits, preferences, and purchasing behavior. This information is crucial for developing effective marketing strategies, optimizing product assortments, and predicting future trends. Advanced use of analytics and machine learning algorithms can further refine companies' ability to make data-driven decisions and personalize offerings.

These dynamics, along with the previous ones, paint a constantly evolving landscape, where the ability to adapt and innovate becomes key to long-term success in the retail sector.

Globalization and Local Adaptation: Retail often operates on a global scale, seeking to expand its presence in new markets. This requires a careful balance between adapting to local preferences and maintaining a consistent brand identity. Companies must navigate different regulations, cultures, and consumer habits, often creating specific product assortments to meet local consumer needs.

Vertical Integration: Vertical integration is another business model many retail companies are adopting. Controlling the entire value chain, from production to distribution to retail, allows greater control over costs, product quality, and availability. This model can also facilitate the implementation of sustainable and ethical practices along the supply chain.

Customer Loyalty and Loyalty Programs: Creating and maintaining customer loyalty is crucial for long-term success. Companies are investing in loyalty programs, offering discounts, rewards, and exclusive benefits to members. Analyzing data collected through these programs can offer valuable insights into consumer behavior and help personalize offers and communications.

Branding and Positioning: Branding is essential for differentiation in a competitive market. Companies significantly invest in building and maintaining a strong brand image that reflects the company's values and value proposition. Strategic market positioning, through defining a specific target demographic and effective communication of differentiation points, is crucial to attracting and retaining customers.

Private Label and Store Brands: The rise of private labels is a significant trend in the retail sector. By creating and selling products under their own brand, companies can offer more competitive prices while maintaining higher profit margins. This allows greater control over quality and production and offers the opportunity to build a direct relationship with consumers.

E-commerce and Logistics: The expansion of e-commerce has demanded an evolution in logistical infrastructures. Companies are developing innovative logistic solutions to manage the challenges of home delivery, such as parcel lockers, drones, and autonomous vehicles. Logistic efficiency is crucial to maintain customer satisfaction and ensure the profitability of online operations.

Creating Unique Shopping Experiences:
To attract consumers to physical stores, retail is experimenting with innovative store formats and creating unique shopping experiences. This may include tasting areas, in-store events, immersive store layouts, and the integration of technologies such as augmented reality.

Regulations and Standards: Finally, companies must confront an increasingly complex and evolving regulatory environment. Adapting to new regulations regarding product labeling, food safety, data protection, and sustainability is essential for effective operation and maintaining consumer trust.

As the retail sector continues to navigate this complex and rapidly evolving landscape, the ability to anticipate changes, adapt, and innovate will remain central to future success.

In conclusion, the retail sector operates in an environment continually shaped by a series of dynamic and interconnected factors. The adoption of innovative business models and competitive strategies is imperative to maintain relevance in the market and effectively meet the continuously evolving needs of consumers.

In particular, companies in the sector must be ready to navigate the challenges and opportunities presented by globalization and local adaptation. Balancing maintaining a consistent brand identity and adapting to the diverse needs of consumers in various markets is a crucial aspect.

The importance of vertical integration, branding, and the development of private labels is also essential for controlling the value chain and differentiation in the market. These elements, along with loyalty programs, play a central role in building and maintaining lasting consumer relationships, while also providing valuable insights for personalized offerings.

With the rise of e-commerce, the retail sector must evolve its logistical infrastructure, developing innovative solutions to meet the growing expectations of consumers for convenience and delivery speed. At the same time, creating unique shopping experiences in physical stores remains fundamental to attract and retain customers.

Finally, adapting to an increasingly complex regulatory environment represents an ongoing challenge. Companies must stay updated and compliant with the latest regulations and standards, thus safeguarding consumer trust and mitigating the risks associated with non-compliance.

In summary, the retail landscape is in continuous transformation, and companies must adopt a proactive and innovative approach to successfully navigate this dynamic environment. The implementation of competitive strategies and flexible business models, along with attention to emerging trends and consumer needs, will be crucial for long-term success in this sector.

30. Customer Service and Complaint Management

Customer Service and Complaint Management are essential components for any company in the retail sector. These functions are vital to maintain customer trust and satisfaction and continually improve the offering of products and services.

Customer Service Customer service represents the primary point of contact between the company and consumers, crucial in building and maintaining positive relationships. Effective customer service should promptly respond to customer queries, resolve issues, provide information and assistance, and manage complaints efficiently and professionally. Modern technologies like chatbots, artificial intelligence, and multichannel communication platforms are revolutionizing how companies interact with customers. Using these tools can enhance the speed and effectiveness of customer service by providing timely responses and personalized solutions.

Training customer service staff is equally important. Employees need to possess the necessary skills to handle a variety of situations and communicate clearly and empathetically.

Complaint Management Complaint management is a specific aspect of customer service that deals with resolving consumer complaints. An effective complaints management system should be able to identify, record, track, and resolve complaints promptly.

It's essential to treat every complaint as a learning opportunity. By analyzing complaint data, companies can identify trends, isolate

problematic areas, and implement corrective measures to prevent future issues.
Additionally, transparency and communication are crucial in the complaint management process. Companies need to keep customers informed about the status of their complaints and the actions taken to resolve them. A good relationship with the customer during this process can strengthen the relationship and enhance the company's reputation.

Conclusions In conclusion, excellent Customer Service and robust Complaint Management are indispensable for customer satisfaction and competitiveness in the retail sector. Investing in qualified personnel, innovative technologies, and efficient processes can significantly contribute to the company's long-term success and its market reputation.

In the current retail landscape, the importance of Customer Service and Complaint Management cannot be overstated. With the growing need for impeccable customer service, companies are exploring new frontiers and adopting innovative strategies.

Customer Service Evolution The evolution of communication channels has expanded the customer service landscape. Social media, for example, has become a key channel for interacting with customers, allowing a direct and bidirectional dialogue. This enables companies to obtain real-time feedback and respond promptly to customer needs.

Personalizing service is another crucial aspect. Ethically using customer data allows companies to offer tailored solutions and anticipate consumer needs, creating a more rewarding and loyal customer experience.

Proactive Complaint Management

Proactively managing complaints is an emerging strategy. Instead of waiting for customers to submit complaints, companies are adopting proactive approaches, actively monitoring social media and other online channels to identify and resolve potential issues before they escalate. Additionally, implementing technology-based complaint management systems allows for quicker and more effective resolution of complaints. Automation can help categorize and forward complaints to the right department, reducing waiting times and improving customer satisfaction.

Continuous Training and Skill Development The importance of continuous staff training cannot be overlooked. With the constant development of new technologies and customer expectations, it's essential for staff to be adequately trained and updated on industry best practices.

Empathy and listening skills are fundamental competencies every customer service representative should possess. Training in these areas can help create a more conducive environment for dialogue and problem resolution, improving the relationship between the company and the customer.

Customer Satisfaction Measurement
Adopting effective methods to measure customer satisfaction is crucial. This can include surveys, interviews, and online data analysis. Understanding what makes customers happy and what can be improved is critical for continuous improvement in customer service and complaint management.
Holistic Approach
Finally, adopting a holistic approach is fundamental. Customer service and complaint management are not isolated but interconnected with other business functions such as marketing, sales, and production. Integration and collaboration among these departments can lead to greater coherence and more effective service. Optimal management of customer service and complaints in retail not only involves implementing innovative strategies and adopting new communication channels but also requires a

deep commitment to performance analysis and continuous improvement.

A crucial aspect in this context is the company's ability to quickly adapt to market trends and changing consumer needs. Adaptability and flexibility are key to maintaining a high level of customer service and effectively managing complaints. Regular assessment of internal procedures and the willingness to update obsolete practices can significantly contribute to this process.

The importance of technology is undeniable in this sphere. Integrating advanced technological solutions, such as AI chatbots and CRM systems, can enhance the responsiveness and efficiency of customer service. However, maintaining a balance between automation and human interaction is also crucial, ensuring that technology does not compromise the quality of the customer relationship.

Additionally, data management plays a central role. Collecting and analyzing customer data not only allows for service personalization but also identifies areas for improvement and predicts future trends. Protecting this data is equally essential, and companies must ensure compliance with privacy regulations and information security.

Employee training and skill development remain fundamental elements. Training must be continuous and updated, covering not only technical skills but also relational and communication skills. Staff should be prepared to handle stressful situations and resolve problems effectively, while maintaining a positive and constructive attitude.

Customer satisfaction measurement, through surveys and feedback, is another cornerstone. Analyzing this data helps understand customer needs, continuously improve services offered, and adapt to market expectations.

Finally, the holistic approach emphasizes the importance of integration and collaboration among various company departments. Consistency among marketing, sales, production, and customer service strategies is essential to provide a consistent and satisfying customer experience.

In conclusion, customer service and complaint management in retail are constantly evolving fields, requiring constant commitment, adoption of advanced technologies, staff training, and careful performance analysis. Only through a holistic approach and continuous focus on innovation and adaptability can companies ensure customer satisfaction and maintain a competitive position in the market.

Throughout this book, we have explored various aspects of the retail sector, offering a comprehensive overview of its different elements and the challenges it faces. We have examined:

1. **History and Development:** The historical evolution of retail and how it has influenced the current landscape of the sector.
2. **Store Formats and Types:** Different formats and business models, highlighting their unique characteristics.
3. **Technology and Digitalization:** The significance of technology, e-commerce, and digitalization in modernizing the industry.
4. **Supply Chain and Logistics:** The complexities of supply chain management and logistical optimization.
5. **Marketing and Advertising:** Essential marketing and advertising strategies to attract and retain customers.
6. **Corporate Social Responsibility:** The growing role of sustainability and ethics in business.
7. **Laws and Regulations:** The laws and regulations governing the sector.
8. **Human Resources:** Human resource management and the importance of staff training.

9. **Crises and Opportunities:** How the sector has faced crises like the COVID-19 pandemic and emerging opportunities.
10. **Product Innovations:** Current trends in new product development.
11. **Packaging and Labeling:** The evolution of packaging and labeling and their impact on consumers.
12. **Future Trends and Perspectives:** Reflection on future trends and perspectives in retail.
13. **Competition and Differentiation:** Growing competition and differentiation strategies.
14. **SWOT Analysis:** Evaluation of the industry's strengths, weaknesses, opportunities, and threats.
15. **Case Studies and Success Stories:** Practical examples of success and lessons learned from failures.
16. **Role of Emerging Technologies:** The impact of new technologies such as Blockchain and AI.
17. **Impact on the Local Community:** How retail affects local communities.
18. **Business Models and Competitive Strategies:** An in-depth analysis of competitive strategies.
19. **Customer Service and Complaint Management:** The importance of effective customer service and complaint management.

For further information and insights, one can visit specialized websites such as:

- **Nielsen:** For market data and analysis (www.nielsen.com).
- **Euromonitor International:** For global market research (www.euromonitor.com).
- **IBISWorld:** For industry reports and market analysis (www.ibisworld.com).
- **Statista:** For market statistics and data (www.statista.com).

Additionally, numerous publications and online guides from sources like Harvard Business Review, Forbes, and Business Insider offer articles and case studies on retail trends and business strategies.
In conclusion, the retail sector is dynamic and continually evolving, and staying informed and updated on these topics is essential for anyone interested in fully understanding its dynamics and future challenges.